Landmarks of Otsego County

A York State Book

Landmarks of Otsego County

DIANTHA DOW SCHULL

Open access edition funded by the National Endowment for the Humanities/Andrew W. Mellon Foundation Humanities Open Book Program.

Copyright © 1980 by Syracuse University Press, Syracuse, New York 13244-5290

All Rights Reserved

First Edition
Second paperback printing, 1981

This book is published with the assistance of a grant from The Nourse Foundation. Winner of the 1980 John Ben Snow Manuscript Prize

Pertinent photographs reproduced courtesy of Mark Zeek, Cooperstown, NY

For a listing of books published and distributed by Syracuse University Press, visit https://press.syr.edu.

ISBN: 978-0-8156-0158-6 (paperback)
ISBN: 978-1-68445-014-5 (e-book)
DOI: https://doi.org/10.14305/sub.hobp.9781684450145

Library of Congress Cataloging-in-Publication Data
Schull, Diantha Dow.
Landmarks of Otsego County
  (A York State book)
  Includes index.
1. Historic buildings—New York (State)—Otsego Co.
2. Otsego Co., N.Y.—History, Local.   3. Architecture—
New York (State)—Otsego Co.   I. Title.
F127.0'93S38   974.7'74   80-11825
ISBN 0-8156-0157-3
ISBN 0-8156-0158-1 (pbk.)

CONTENTS

Preface   ix
1. Architectural Forms   1
    Regional Variations on Formal Styles   1
    Construction Materials   2
    Early Settlement   3
    Federal   10
    Greek Revival   13
    Gothic Revival   18
    Italianate   20
    Second Empire   23
    Pictorial Eclectic   30
    Queen Anne and Shingle   32
    Romanesque   34
    Neo-Classical Revival   37
2. Towns and Villages, Historic Districts, and Rural Landmarks   39
3. The Lake Region   43
    Town of Springfield   45
    Town of Richfield   51
    Village of Richfield Springs   52

  Town of Exeter   59
  Town of Otsego   64
  Village of Cooperstown   70
  Farmers' Museum and Village Crossroads   92

4. Upper Unadilla Valley   96
  Town of Plainfield   97
  Town and Village of Edmeston   102
  Town of Pittsfield   106

5. Butternut Creek Valley   111
  Town of Burlington   112
  Town of New Lisbon   116
  Town of Morris   122
  Village of Morris   125
  Town of Butternuts   134
  Village of Gilbertsville   136

6. Upper Susquehanna River Basin   148
  Town of Hartwick   151
  Town and Village of Laurens   163
  Town of Milford   171
  Town of Oneonta   176
  City of Oneonta and the Walnut Street Historic District   179
  Town and Village of Otego   198
  Town of Unadilla   203
  Village of Unadilla   207

7. Schenevus Creek Valley   221
    Town of Maryland   222
    Town of Worcester   232
    The Worcester Historic District   238
8. Cherry Valley Region   247
    Towns of Roseboom and Westford   248
    Town of Middlefield   254
    Town of Cherry Valley   260
    Village of Cherry Valley   262
9. Preservation in Otsego County   274
    Index   277

Diantha Dow Schull is museum coordinator for the Museum Aid Program for the New York State Council on the Arts and was a consultant in history and preservation in the Upper Catskill region. She lives with her family in an early nineteenth-century farmhouse in Laurens, in Otsego County.

PREFACE

OTSEGO COUNTY contains an abundance of buildings of both visual and historic interest. Some of them have outstanding architectural merit, while others are modest structures expressive of local traditions and resources. All are important to the local landscape and thus are considered landmarks. This book is intended as a record and appreciation of some of these landmarks as well as a catalyst for expanding awareness of the overall architectural heritage of the county.

Until recently only formally designed structures, particularly the homes of important people, were considered worthy of documentation and preservation. Few historians, architects, or preservationists acknowledged the value of less prominent buildings, the homes of ordinary citizens, or the utilitarian structures. There is now, however, increasing recognition that local structures contribute as much to the character of an area as do the major monuments, and for this reason I have tried to identify vernacular buildings, regional variations on accepted architectural styles.

Inevitably many significant structures have not been included in this book. Because it is a selective listing, for every building mentioned here there are two or three others of equal interest, particularly in the rural areas. Time and space constraints limited the scope of the book to those structures still standing and in a few instances those recently demolished. The same considerations prevented attention to the interiors of the landmarks.

Otsego County is rich in sources for the architectural historian or student of material culture. Future studies should examine the contemporary environment, for historic structures do not exist in isolation but are part of an evolving landscape. If as a result of this book further studies are undertaken, it will have served an important purpose.

The landmarks have been grouped by regions which have a natural identity due to architectural, topographical, or historic characteristics. Within each region descriptions of the buildings are arranged for walking or driving ease. Using the map as a guide, the traveler can follow the sequence of entries in the book or select specific sections to explore in depth. The main roads traversing the different regions usually link major villages; the reader is encouraged to examine each of these villages as well as to seek out the rural landmarks which are accessible on smaller roads.

In exploring the county's landmarks the reader is also encouraged to observe them in relation to other features of the landscape, for they are only one element of the special character of Otsego County.

This book could not have been completed without the cooperation and assistance so generously given by the owners and occupants of the buildings discussed here. I am also indebted to the many local historians who contributed information and corrected me on points of local history.

Certain individuals have given freely of their time and expertise or have provided invaluable moral support, among them Hannah and George Benedict, Harriet and John Dow, Colonel Joy Wheeler Dow, Dr. Louis C. Jones, Jack Erikson, Jonathan Gell, Evelyn Lower, Ann Gilbert Mangold, Doris Manly, Frederick Rath, Dorothy and Leonard Ryndes, and Margaret Schneider. An indirect influence on the study has been my paternal grandfather, Joy Wheeler Dow, author, builder, and critic, who would no doubt quarrel with some of my judgments.

The majority of the illustrations are by Mark Zeek, whose sensitivity to the architectural qualities of the region is reflected in his photographic work. The remainder of the photographs are by myself or Eric S. Allegretti. Robert Hage contributed plate 201 and the Oneonta *Daily Star* plate 159.

I gratefully acknowledge the financial support of The Nourse Foundation and the New York State Council on the Arts (Architecture and Environmental Arts Program), as well as the sponsorship of the Upper Catskill Community Council on the Arts.

The fullest acknowledgment is due my husband, Walter B. Schull, without whose insights and assistance this book would never have been completed.

Laurens, New York
Summer 1979

Diantha Dow Schull

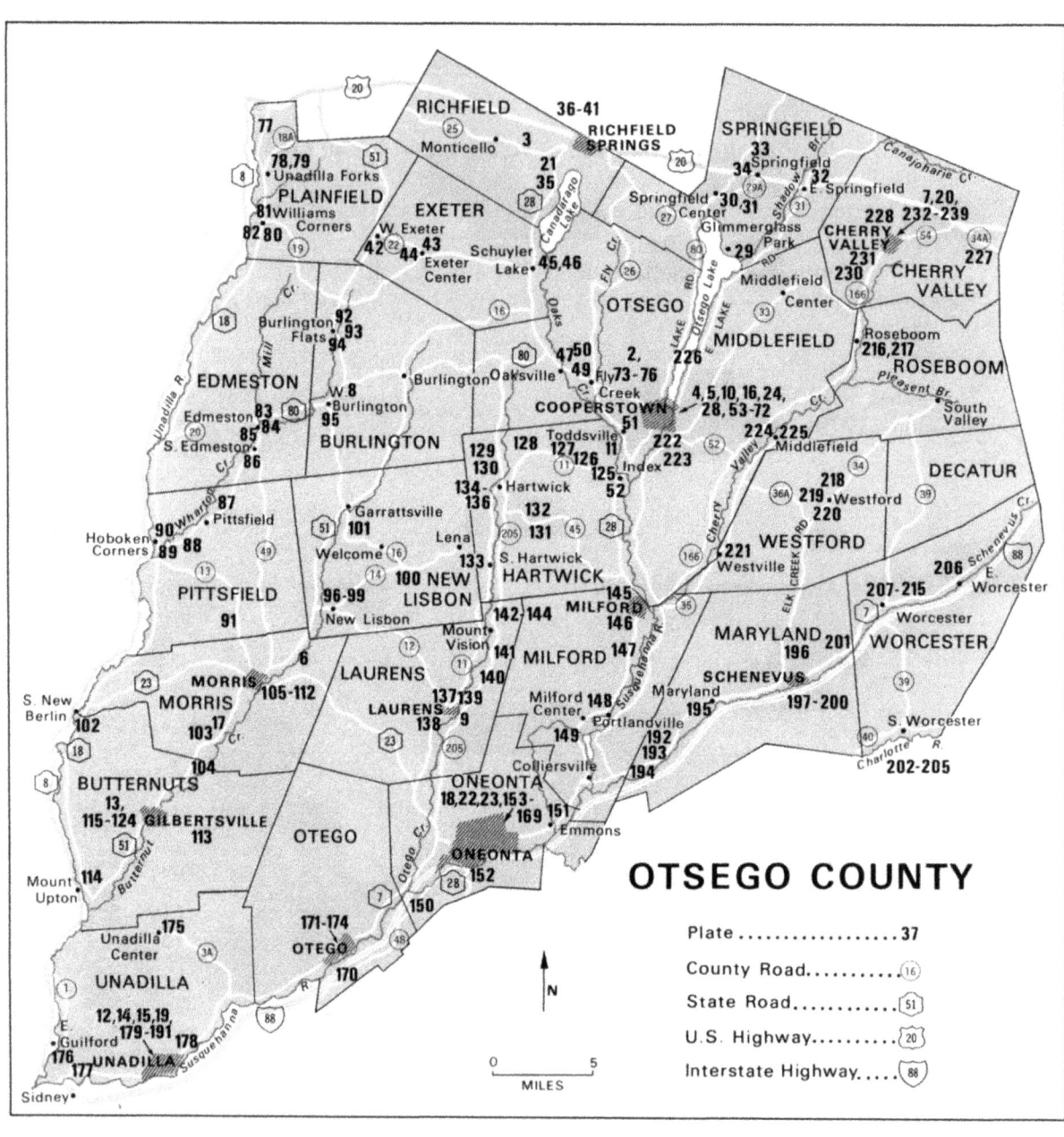

Landmarks of Otsego County

1

ARCHITECTURAL FORMS

Regional Variations on Formal Styles

THE ARCHITECTURE OF OTSEGO COUNTY before the twentieth century followed styles developed largely in Britain and in the urban centers of New England and the eastern seaboard. While it is useful to refer to the sequence of common national styles, rigid classification is usually misleading if not impossible. Stylistic periods do not have sharp edges. Pure designations of buildings can be hampered by unusual combinations of stylistic elements, by later additions, or by the fact that there could be a twenty- to thirty-year lag before a style became fashionable.

Stylistic analysis does not usually take account of the regional variations on accepted forms which distinguish buildings in such areas as Otsego County. Any characterization of architectural developments in the county must therefore convey the wide range of variations possible within the time-frame for each stylistic period: "vernacular" buildings are local interpretations of currently popular styles; "transitional" buildings embody characteristics of a recently popular style plus those of current styles; and "referential" buildings employ contemporary interpretations of a historic or no longer popular style. Only through an awareness of these variations can the distinctive structures which constitute the local landscape be fully appreciated.

The majority of buildings in Otsego County are vernacular, local and personal variations on the historical styles which satisfied functional and aesthetic needs. These were produced anonymously, either by owner-builders or by community "housewrights." Very few buildings in the county were professionally designed, particularly in the first half of the nineteenth century. It is possible that local craftsmen had access to architectural pattern books which were circulating quite early in the century. However, even buildings in which "period" styles have been faithfully copied have a local originality of detail and proportion, such as the Dr. Greenough House (plate 125) and All Saints Chapel (plate 104).

Construction Materials

Many of the historic buildings in Otsego County were constructed of wood — white pine, ash, cedar, and oak — the most plentiful resource and the material with which most settlers were familiar. Other construction materials were used intermittently, including fieldstone, brick, limestone, and granite. (A farmhouse in the Springfield area, remodeled now, is reported to have interior walls of adobe.)

Stone houses are found throughout the county, particularly at its western edge. Some of these have elaborate masonry, a tradition more popular in western sections of New York State. There are very few cobblestone structures in Otsego County (plate 42), but numerous cobblestone barn basements are located in the western and northern townships. Limestone is found in the northern and northeastern parts of the county, hence the many limestone buildings in and near Cherry Valley (plate 235). Bricks were made and used locally on occasion, but with the ready access to timber large-scale manufacture of bricks was not emphasized. It was not until the late nineteenth century, with the mass manufacture and transportation of brick, that it became more commonly used in the construction of large homes and public buildings (plate 156).

Early Settlement

Before the American Revolution the region of present-day Otsego County was occupied by scattered Indian tribes and a few white settlers. Several important Indian village sites have been identified within the boundaries of the county. During the eighteenth century a handful of explorers and surveyors toured the area with a view to possible settlement. The land then was divided into patents or sections of patents allocated to nonresidents with political and familial connections. Actual settlers subsequently purchased lots in those patents. No buildings from that period have survived.

By the time of the Fort Stanwix Treaty in 1768 several sections of the county were sparsely populated. The first settlement was at the site of the present village of Cherry Valley, where a group of Scotch-Irish settled in 1740. Soon after, settlements occurred in Morris, with a group from Orange County, and later French émigrés, and in the township of Worcester, where German-Dutch families settled along the Charlotte River. Other small settlements sprang up in the townships of Hartwick, Edmeston, Otsego, and Laurens before the Revolutionary War.

During the Revolution residents of these early settlements fled the area or took refuge in the stockade at Cherry Valley. Homes left behind were destroyed by Indians loyal to the British; no extant buildings have yet been documented as dating from before the Revolution.

The first landmarks of Otsego County were constructed when permanent settlements were started between 1780 and 1800. Some families and soldiers returned to their former locations to rebuild and to take advantage of the abundant and fertile land. A wave of settlers soon followed. In 1786 William Cooper came from New Jersey to develop the area around present-day Cooperstown; in 1791 the New York State legislature officially created Otsego County from sections of twelve earlier counties; and in 1800 the Catskill Turnpike was chartered and extended to its western terminus at Unadilla, the junction of the Susquehanna and Unadilla rivers.

During the first years settlers encountered grave hardships and had few comforts. Housing consisted of crude shelters, often of logs, built to serve immediate needs. If any of these first dwellings remain, they have been rewalled and remodeled beyond recognition. The only log structure visible today is the log barn at the Farmers' Museum in Cooperstown (plate 76). A few buildings can be dated with certainty before 1800 (plate 59), but the majority of historic buildings date from the nineteenth century.

The earliest buildings were generally rudimentary dwellings, small and functional, or agricultural buildings which have since been re-used for a variety of purposes. These first homes varied in size from one- or two-room cottages to large versions of the saltbox style, characterized by the long slope of the roof from front to rear. It was not uncommon for a lean-to to be built later on the original building for extra space. These early buildings were usually one or one-and-one-half stories with large central or end chimneys. Openings and doors were simply framed; little attention was paid to decorative detail. It was not until people prospered that they began to embellish structures with artistic motifs.

Early homesteads may be found throughout the county, but most have been enlarged and remodeled to the extent that their original forms are virtually unrecognizable. Often the only observable feature which survives is the outline of the roof extending to cover the lean-to addition at the rear.

Established residents later enlarged their original homes or constructed more permanent homesteads. Some of these can be dated before 1800, but the majority were erected in the first decade of the nineteenth century. These larger buildings borrowed from the Georgian tradition. The proportions were substantial, the details straightforward and rich with some classical overtones. Most of the homesteads were two-and-one-half stories with medium-pitched gable or hipped roofs, usually inset chimneys, a symmetrical façade with center door, and rectangular, small-paned windows. The earliest taverns, which were constructed to accommodate a rapid growth in traffic westward, also exhibited these Georgian features.

1. LOG HOUSE, Town of Maryland. Although no residential buildings constructed of logs are visible in Otsego County, it is likely that they do exist, obscured by later siding and additions. This building was photographed in 1889 by Fred Beach of Oneonta; his description reads: "a scene near Colliersville." The structure has characteristics similar to Levi Beardsley's description in *Reminiscences* of the log house his father had erected in 1790 on their newly purchased lot in Richfield Springs:

> The one that we moved in . . . was a small log cabin, the body laid up, and part, though not the whole of the roof was covered with black ash and elm bark. . . . The floor was made of bass wood logs, split and hewed partially on one side, and then spotted down, making a good substantial floor. . . . A place for the door was cut out, so that we could go in, but no door had been made, nor had we any way of fastening the door except by barricading. . . . A mud and stick chimney and fireplace were afterwards added, as the weather became cool.

Based on this description and others of early log homes in Otsego County and adjacent areas of Central New York, the scene in Colliersville must have been a typical one.

2. LIPPITT FARMHOUSE, Farmers' Museum, Lake Road, Cooperstown.
A central feature of the re-created village at the Farmers' Museum is the farmhouse built about 1797 by Joseph Lippitt on land procured from Judge Cooper. Originally located in the town of Hartwick (Hinman Hollow), the Lippitt home was removed to the museum to represent the type of frontier framstead common in the Upper Susquehanna region after 1800. The saltbox silhouette of the building, with its lean-to at the rear, the simple corner posts, the simply framed doorway with headlight, and the central chimney are all characteristic features of the homes of the earliest settlers in Otsego County.

3. **MILLER TAVERN, Route 25, between Richfield Springs and Monticello, Town of Richfield.** As settlement increased in the Otsego Lake region, passenger traffic necessitated the construction of taverns along the plank roads or turnpikes. Remaining taverns are vivid reminders of the period of early settlement. The earliest taverns, like the early permanent homesteads, were plain but substantial in plan. Their structural forms derived from the eighteenth-century Georgian style. The Miller Tavern, constructed in the late eighteenth century on the route of the Skaneateles Turnpike running westward from Richfield Springs, has basic Georgian features: two and one-half stories, massive central chimney, and a balanced façade and center door. The original windows unfortunately have not survived.

4, 5. POMEROY PLACE, 11 Main Street, Cooperstown. Judge William Cooper, founder of Cooperstown, built the first stone house in the village when his daughter Ann married George Pomeroy in 1804. James Allen, "Scotch Jamie" mentioned in James Fenimore Cooper's *Wyandotte*, was the stonemason; the unusual herringbone pattern is charac-

teristic of his work (plate 51). In *The Legends and Traditions of a Northern County* James Fenimore Cooper records the detailed contract between Judge Cooper and the carpenter, Cyrenus Clark, who received $500 for the construction "from the bottom of the seller to the turning of the Key of the Front Door" of this residence.

Federal

The great mass of settlers came into the county during the first quarter of the nineteenth century. Between 1800 and 1820 the population jumped from approximately 21,000 to 45,000 people. The general movement westward accounted for a large percentage of new settlers, while the development of major post routes and turnpikes made the entire Central New York region more accessible.

Most of the settlers were from New England and brought with them the architectural forms with which they were familiar. The homes, churches, and public buildings constructed in the first decades of the nineteenth century have the graceful details and sense of balance associated with the Federal style. It was during this period that carpenters' and builders' handbooks began to be widely circulated. Such a guide as Asher Benjamin's *The American Builder's Companion* may well have been known to housewrights at the beginning of the century.

Federal buildings were rectangular, with low-pitched roofs, or square with hipped roofs. End-wall chimneys were common. Semi-elliptical transoms and sidelights emphasized the central entranceway; small windows of geometric shapes decorated the gables of Federal structures.

The style appeared in simple, country versions throughout the county, with careful proportions, fan and oval arched entranceways, and delicate details. There are also a number of significant examples of the style in more complex form, with detailed entablatures, recessed arches, and Palladian windows (plate 172). Obviously these were constructed by local craftsmen of outstanding native ability who were able to overcome limitations of training and equipment to build sophisticated Federal structures.

6. PEGG HOUSE, Pegg Road, between Morris and New Lisbon, Town of Morris.
This vernacular dwelling is typical of homes built throughout the countryside during the Federal period. The facade is symmetrical; the moldings are simple and restrained; and an arched fanlight appears over the door below a Palladian window characteristic of the period.

7. **Delos White House, 41 Main Street, Cherry Valley.** This residence was constructed approximately 1810 and has been owned by prominent Cherry Valley citizens, including Dr. Delos White and Colonel Samuel Clyde. A central unit flanked by symmetrical wings was a Georgian plan; here it is combined with delicate details and a vertical emphasis characteristic of the Federal style. Note the wide, low-pitched gable and the classical treatment of the pediment.

Greek Revival

Between 1820 and 1840 the population of Otsego County again doubled, accompanied by a great burst of building activity. Communities which had formerly been clusters of modest homes blossomed into market villages with substantial public buildings and small industries.

A large proportion of the extant historic architecture in Otsego County dates from this time of rapid growth. The stylistic preference is obvious: Greek Revival prevailed. Based on design precedents of ancient Greece, Greek Revival buildings may be recognized by their solid appearance and the emphasis on columns or pilasters. They often had triangular pediments or pedimented façades, and Greek motifs were used for ornamentation. Other typical elements include strong entablatures, heavy cornices, plain surfaces, and simple lines. The two typical Greek Revival house plans were the temple-front house with corner pilasters or columns, and the two-story structure with a single one-story wing. One-and-one-half-story residences were also popular, many of them incorporating a row of small windows under the eaves.

The overriding influence of the Greek Revival style was the result of a combination of factors: a period of increasing settlement and economic growth, a national sentiment in favor of the Greek Revolution, and the adoption of Greek forms as the appropriate expression of American democratic ideals and institutions. The Greek Revival was adapted for residential and public use by all those who could afford to do so in American society. The local countryside became studded with modified temple buildings, usually in wood but in brick or stone as well, built for all purposes — residences, stores, grange halls, even barns.

Not all observers of American building applauded the extensive use of Greek forms. James Fenimore Cooper, who spent much of his life at his family home in Cooperstown, observed in his novel *Home as Found*:

8. **GREEK REVIVAL FARMHOUSE, Route 80, Near Junction with Route 51, Town of Burlington.** The common characteristics of the Greek Revival period are exemplified by this simple farmstead, built about 1830. The house plan is a typical one for Otsego County: a temple-front main unit with one side wing. Other features are also typical of Greek Revival structures both large and small: a symmetrical façade; recessed doorway with sidelights; pilasters; broad, flat entablature; a heavy return at the eaves; dentils; and eyebrow windows cut into the classical molding on the long sides.

> An extraordinary taste is afflicting this country in the way of architecture... nothing but a Grecian temple being now deemed a suitable residence for a man in these classical times.... The malady has affected the whole nation.... One such temple well placed in the wood, might be a pleasant object enough; but to see a river lined with them, with children trundling hoops before their doors, beef carried into their kitchens, and smoke issuing, moreover, from those unclassical objects, is too much even for a high taste.

Greek Revival remained popular in the United States until the Civil War. In Otsego County the style was used over a period of four decades. Later examples were heavier in feel and larger in proportion than the early examples. Some later Greek buildings combined elements of the numerous Victorian styles which were becoming fashionable after mid-century. These transitional structures, which fall outside any strict stylistic category, are sometimes the most imaginative and visually interesting (plate 194).

After the opening of the Erie Canal in 1825 transportation and commercial activities tended to bypass the country south of the Mohawk Valley, with a resulting halt in the growth of local industries and market towns. Communities in Otsego County remained relatively stable until the third quarter of the nineteenth century, a condition reflected in the smaller number of extant structures from mid-century, as opposed to the Greek Revival period.

9. **MAPLEHURST OR AUGUSTINE HOUSE, Detail of Capital, Junction of Route 11 and Route 11A, Laurens.** Much ornamental variation occurred within the Greek Revival format. The detail of this Ionic capital, with typical egg-and-dart and rolled acanthus leaf motifs, reveals the work of a skillful craftsman, and one who undoubtedly had access to formal pattern-book guides. Maplehurst is a massive Greek structure, atypically surmounted by a cupola, and has long been a local landmark, serving as the home of prominent Laurens citizens since the 1830s. At one time it was splendidly kept, with showplace gardens. It is currently being renovated for use as an apartment building.

10. LEATHERSTOCKING CORPORATION (formerly the OTSEGO COUNTY BANK), 19 Main Street, Cooperstown. Dignified, solid, carefully proportioned, the Greek Revival style was adopted throughout the county as particularly suitable for commercial and public buildings. One of the most sophisticated examples of classical design in Otsego County is the bank building constructed in Cooperstown in 1831, whose portico resembles those of more grand structures in New York City and Philadelphia. First known as the Otsego County Bank, in 1866 it merged with the National Bank, and still later, in 1897, became the offices of the Clark Foundation. Throughout the county simple frame structures similar in form to this important example may be found (plate 218).

11. GOTHIC REVIVAL RESIDENCE, County Route 26, Toddsville.
The Gothic influence affected Otsego County as it did other sections of Central New York. During the 1840s small picturesque cottages were built which emphasized trefoil tracery and medieval motifs. This Gothic cottage has retained most of its original features: the asymmetrical arrangement, pierced wooded bargeboards, steep gables and verge poles, drip hood molding around the windows, and the bay window.

Gothic Revival

During the 1840s and 1850s there was a wave of interest in romantic and picturesque elements and proportions associated with medieval buildings. Most local Gothic Revival structures are free interpretations of these elements in wood, utilizing the newly developed scroll saw. The resulting buildings are

12. GOTHIC RESIDENCE, 2 Cottage Lane, Unadilla. The kind of ornamental woodwork found on this house is particularly vulnerable. Many Gothic structures which once had such trim have had their wooden tracery destroyed or removed.

distinguished by gingerbread trim, bargeboard ornamentation, steeply pitched gables, pointed-arch openings, and above all an emphasis on vertical lines. Simple examples of the Gothic Revival, many of which have unfortunately had their trim removed, are scattered throughout the county, as are more elaborate examples. The style persisted through the nineteenth century as being appropriate for ecclesiastical use (plate 104).

13. HARRINGTON HOUSE, 30 Spring Street, Gilbertsville. Italianate buildings, characterized by simple cubical shapes and flat or low-pitched roofs with decorative cornice brackets, are seen in both formal and vernacular versions in all areas of the county. Built in the late 1850s, this dwelling is a well-preserved example of the style with its octagonal columns supporting the one-story bracketed porch, the paired brackets themselves, and the overall asymmetrical plan. Often seen, as well, are one- or two-story bay windows.

Italianate

The Italianate style, inspired by large country villas in Tuscany, overlapped the Gothic Revival. The angular forms of the Italian villa were adapted for wood, sometimes stone, and became quite popular in the county about the mid-nineteenth century.

Italianate buildings were asymmetrically arranged rectangular or square blocks, and they featured flat or low-pitched roofs with overhanging eaves decorated by prominent brackets, tall, narrow windows, round-headed window

14. COMMUNITY HOUSE, Main Street, Unadilla. One variation on the Italianate villa is the Venetian villa, in which one rectilinear block is surmounted by the usual projecting eaves and decorative brackets. The former Sperry House in Unadilla is an imposing example. With its two-story bay, tall, narrow double-arched windows and bracketed hood moldings, intact porch, and richly turned brackets, it stands as a strong visual element in the commercial section of the village.

and door openings, balconies, cupolas, and square towers. There are both simple and elaborate variations on the style in Otsego County. Along the main streets of most villages formal Italianate residences exhibit an extraordinary diversity of bracket designs, window openings, and other decorative details. Vernacular versions, somewhat plainer, are prevalent in the countryside.

15. **Brackets and Decorative Scrollwork, Italianate Residence, 60 Main Street, Unadilla.** While many Italianate Otsego County buildings have ornate brackets, these are unusual in form.

16. **SUMMERS HOUSE, 1 Elk Street, Cooperstown.** Built in 1870 in the Second Empire style, this house has retained the exterior details characteristic of the mansard era. The strong slope of the slate roof is emphasized by the addition of decorative dormers and a heavily molded cornice. The bay windows and asymmetrical porch are also common elements of the style.

Second Empire

Second Empire buildings, with their mansard roofs named after the seventeenth-century French architect François Mansart, were characterized by the distinctive roofline with a long slope allowing for extra space on the top floor

17. WHEELER HOUSE PORCH, Route 51, between Morris and Gilbertsville.
The hood which projects over the entranceway to this house is distinctive, with a strong flare at the cornice and robustly scrolled support brackets.

—a feature which American travelers in Europe associated with Paris. Projecting dormers and towers were common features of the style, as was ornamental ironwork known as "cresting." Brackets under overhanging eaves were still in use. Bay windows became popular and were often added to older dwellings. Mansard roofs became so popular that they were applied to other forms, such as the octagonal Bull House in Oneonta (plate 168).

With the conclusion of the Civil War and the introduction of the railroad into the county, the region experienced a new wave of prosperity and building. The economy of the county was enormously affected by railroad activity. Some products manufactured locally began to be produced on a larger scale. In Cooperstown there was a great increase in population and marketing activity; an important creamery expanded in Unadilla; Pineapple Cheese was made in Milford; a cheese factory expanded in West Exeter; cigar manufacturing started in Oneonta; and hops were grown in the rest of the county. The success of these ventures would have been impossible without the railroad.

Parallel to this economic activity were major developments in architecture. There was a proliferation of building fashions, combinations of decorative motifs, and attempts at new forms of construction. A myriad of styles, often loosely termed "Victorian," came into vogue in quick succession. There is no one Victorian style; numerous late nineteenth-century forms reflect the eclectic tastes of the period. Similarly, there are few pure examples of any one style; rather, most buildings from the 1870s through the turn of the century exemplify the Victorian principle of mixing motifs and forms.

During the late Victorian era a general spirit of experimentation, the availability of new building techniques, and an individualistic and romantic mood contributed to the erection of unconventional structures. The octagonal style was the best known and oddest of the Victorian experiments. At least seven examples survive in Otsego County.

18. **Delaware and Hudson Railway Company Roundhouse, Oneonta.**
The D & H Roundhouse symbolizes the significance of Oneonta and Otsego County as a center of railroad activity. By 1900 more than 600 men were employed at the D & H yards. When erected in 1906, this building was the largest roundhouse in the world and included 522 stalls, a 75-foot turntable, and a coaling trestle. In 1920–24 it was enlarged further. Unfortunately, the structure is in semiruins, although other nineteenth-century buildings in the D & H railroad yards are still functioning.

19. **1879 Block, Main Street, Unadilla.** Some of the communities in the Upper Susquehanna and Schenevus Creek valleys which grew rapidly during the railroad era have retained their commercial sections, buildings mainly of brick but often frame, which were constructed to house a growing number of shops, offices, and other public functions. This row in Unadilla, with its patterned brick cornices, series of arched windows, unaltered store fronts and complex roof lines, exemplifies the kinds of late nineteenth-century commercial structures which lined the county's main streets.

20. DOUBLE HOP HOUSE (now destroyed), Route 166, Cherry Valley.
The extension of railroad lines into Otsego County made possible widespread marketing of local agricultural products. Toward the end of the century one of the most important of these products was hops, the basic ingredient for the manufacture of beer. Now rare, hop houses were once a common feature of the rural landscape. This unusual double hop structure was recently destroyed by arson.

21. BAKER OCTAGONAL BARN, Route 28, South of Richfield Springs.
The large eight-sided barn built by the Baker family in 1882 is one of at least seven surviving examples of octagonal buildings in Otsego County, and one of two such barns. The octagonal form seemed well suited for agricultural use: this barn was constructed on three levels, each of which could be entered at grade. Cows stood in a circle facing the center and were fed efficiently from above.

Pictorial Eclectic

The architectural character of Otsego County was strongly influenced in the last three decades of the century by a style broadly termed Pictorial Eclectic. The basic premise of this style was an irregular massing of elements, while specific detailing revealed numerous and varied sources. A mélange of architectural details — classical columns, Renaissance balconies, French mansard roofs, and Gothic turrets — worked in brick, shingle, or tile were added in delightful confusion to buildings that are, as a consequence, difficult to classify but wonderful to observe. The style is characterized by its exterior embellishments and curious shapes. Typical features include an asymmetrical plan, prominent and curvacious brackets, brick patterning, intricate lathe and scroll saw-designed woodwork, bay windows, and iron grillwork on roof peaks. Flamboyant in its extreme versions, restless and decorative in its simpler forms, the style was embraced by newly successful politicians and businessmen as an appropriate expression of their prosperity and optimism. Exceptional examples of the style appear in those villages which saw much building activity following on the railroad, such as Cooperstown and Richfield Springs.

22. **ALBERT MORRIS HOUSE, 43 Walnut Street, Walnut Street Historic District, Oneonta.** In the late nineteenth century prominent residents of the communities which were prospering due to the railroad constructed homes which reflected their new aspirations and status, often in the Pictorial Eclectic style. This extravagant home was built by Oneonta's first mayor, Albert Morris, in 1885–86. Morris was engaged in a highly successful feed business; his three sons, also business associates, all built substantial homes nearby on Walnut Street (see the section on the Walnut Street Historic

District). The structure has a restlessness and vitality characteristic of the style which is expressed in its diverse elements: in the thrust of the hipped roof and gables, the extra chimneys, the Second Empire tower with mansard roof, and the asymmetry of the wrap-around porches. The mix of stylistic influences also characteristic of the style is seen in the Stick style detailing, the classical dentils, the Shingle style hooded dormer, the Ionic columns, and the Gothic trefoil window. Now converted for use as a nursing home, this is one of the most picturesque elements in the Walnut Street Historic District.

23. 11, 13 WALNUT STREET, Walnut Street Historic District, Oneonta.
There are numerous examples in the county of simple residences built with Queen Anne or Shingle style features. These two in the Walnut Street Historic District in Oneonta were designed by Oneonta architect Lyman Blend in 1896–97.

Queen Anne and Shingle

The most popular design for domestic architecture at the turn of the century, the romantic Queen Anne style was pseudo-medieval in form. While the architectural detailing is less elaborate than on buildings in the Pictorial Eclectic mode, a variety of patterns, textures, and shapes were employed to create complex structures. Distinguishing features were nonsymmetrical composition, intersecting gables, round or polygonal towers, bay windows, leaded and stained glass, and varied surface textures with delicately turned spindle work and walls often sheathed in wooden shingles. The Shingle and Eastlake styles, which occurred simultaneously, emphasized one or another of these aspects but were generally similar in plan and inspiration. The variations which developed in the county reflected local tastes as well as builders' skills.

24. FORESTVIEW, 41 Nelson Avenue, Cooperstown. Both the Queen Anne and Shingle styles were popular locally during the 1890s, and structures often combined elements of the two. Built in 1892, Forestview was styled after plans for a Queen Anne home advertised in the *Architects and Builders Edition of the Scientific American Magazine* (May 1891). It is an excellent example of the style with the typical irregular plan, projecting walls and dormers, intersecting gables, wrap-around porch, and conical tower. The use of a variety of surface materials (small shingles, wooden strips) to create different textures is also typical of the Shingle style.

Romanesque

There are unfortunately very few surviving examples of the distinctive Romanesque style in Otsego County. Characterized by massive masonry construction resembling European fortifications, the style was also known as Richardsonian, after H. H. Richardson, the architect who popularized designs based on European Romanesque forms. Romanesque buildings were generally large, built for public or educational functions. The county's most outstanding example, "Old Main" or the Old State Normal School in Oneonta, was demolished in 1977.

25, 26. OLD MAIN, State Street, Oneonta. Some good examples of the Romanesque style in Otsego County have unfortunately been destroyed. "Old Main" was demolished in 1977. Built in 1894–95 by the Albany architect Albert Fuller, of the firm of Fuller and Wheeler, it was an outstanding example of Richardsonian Romanesque architecture. There are few examples locally or statewide of the scope and detail of "Old Main," which was conspicuous for its mass, three large entrance arches, the rhythmic parade of arcaded windows, and the combination of colors and textures on the façade. Sited on a hill overlooking Oneonta, the huge (160 rooms) structure was well known to residents, former students, and visitors. "Old Main" was the first structure of the Oneonta Normal School, which later became a part of the State University of New York. As such it stood as a monument to the importance of education in the city's development and in retrospect as an achievement of unequalled architectural excellence in the county.

27. **River Street Primary School, River Street, Oneonta.** This fine example of the large Romanesque school structures built toward the turn of the century unfortunately was demolished in 1974.

Neo-Classical Revival

At about the turn of the century there was a reaction against the freedom of expression which had come to characterize the eclectic building fashions in the previous three decades. Conservative architects sought to return to more traditional forms of the eighteenth century. Picturesque elements were rejected in favor of symmetry and classical order for which there was historical precedent. Neo-Classical Revival buildings were generally monumental in scale, which made the style particularly suitable for important public buildings. Residences built in this mode were often the large homes of prominent citizens (plate 197).

Since 1900 development in Otsego County has remained relatively stable. Rapid industrialization after the railroad meant the demise of some communities as economic centers. The influence of Oneonta as an educational and marketing center has increased along with the general decline of the dairy industry, formerly the backbone of the economy.

There has been a general shift in population from the rural sections of the county toward the more developed southeastern section, near the city of Oneonta. Rural structures have been increasingly abandoned, and formerly vital hamlets and villages have become less important as commercial centers.

The architectural features of the county today record these changes. Historic buildings still constitute the bulk of the county's structural resources, with new construction limited mainly to the southeastern portions of the county. With due recognition and adequate planning these buildings will continue to contribute to the special character of the area.

28. COOPERSTOWN MUNICIPAL BUILDING, 22 Main Street, Cooperstown.
As the end of the century neared builders returned to the use of classical elements, often elaborately detailed and executed on a massive scale. The Cooperstown Municipal Building was designed by Ernest Flagg of New York City in 1896–97. In style it bears a close relationship to the nearby Baseball Hall of Fame and the Alfred Corning Clark Gymnasium, all of which have large-scale classical details. The tall white Corinthian columns and the breadth of the building make it a commanding element on Main Street.

2

TOWNS AND VILLAGES, HISTORIC DISTRICTS, AND RURAL LANDMARKS

THE MAJORITY OF OTSEGO COUNTY LANDMARKS are located in the small villages and hamlets that still form the basis of the region's social and economic activity. Despite increasingly disruptive forces in recent decades, the county's many villages and hamlets retain strong identities and continue to serve as the focus of community life for their own and outlying residents. With an abundance of historic structures, they constitute a series of environmental groupings deserving of recognition and protection. The fact that contemporary activities continue within these genuine historic settings underscores their significance as living museums. No artificially created environment, no deliberately assembled "historic village," can have the aesthetic or historic impact that these communities naturally possess.

The structural features of Otsego County villages reflect a sequence of settlement, movement of population, stabilization of community life, and subsequent economic pressures. Many of the villages have remained essentially unchanged in population and in structural appearance since the time of their greatest development in the mid- or late nineteenth century. In some cases there has been a decline in population with a resulting overall deterioration and/or abandonment of historic structures. Between the end of the last century and the late 1960s there was little growth in the county; since then, only limited development has occurred.

The proportion of extant structures associated with various historical periods provides clues as to the development of a community. In the former mill villages, such as Laurens and Fly Creek, development stopped in the mid-nineteenth century after the Erie Canal farther north attracted most of the industrial and transportation activity. In these towns Greek Revival forms predominate. In other villages, such as Edmeston and Schenevus, decline did not occur until after the peak of railroad activity early in the 1900s. Here the later Victorian styles, such as the Pictorial Eclectic and Queen Anne, are well represented.

The exact makeup of the village settings in the county varies considerably depending upon their particular developmental patterns. However, the following types of structures appear in almost every community. Churches were one of the earliest and most prominent features of village settings. Agricultural structures are special landmarks in that they have provided the basis for economic life in the county and are especially rooted in the traditional practices of their owner/builders. Commercial buildings provide a record of local economic activity. Public buildings are important for an understanding of political and administrative changes. Educational buildings are records of cultural and educational ambitions and standards. Industrial buildings reflect industrial and product development in the county. Transportation structures are related to settlement patterns and changes in communications. Dwellings illustrate more than any of the other building types the changing fashions in building-design and life styles. The special character of each community is determined by the relationship of these building types to one another and to the surrounding environmental features.

The plan or layout of each community also contributes to its particular identity. Certain villages retain evidences of a common green, an open space around which buildings were constructed. This green, or village square, was the common plan utilized in New England towns and was retained by settlers as they moved westward. Richfield Springs, Burlington Green, and the village green in Gilbertsville are examples of this tradition.

Most Otsego County villages grew up around one main street with adjacent streets laid out as required later. This plan suited the needs of the developing settlements; growth was uneven and one main artery allowed for expansion along either side. In Unadilla, for instance, Main Street ran roughly parallel to the Susquehanna River and was extended to reach more than a mile with churches, homes, taverns, and shops facing on the street. This was the case as well in Worcester, with commercial activity centered at one end of the street and residences concentrated at the other end.

Another typical village plan in the county is the "four corners," where community life is focused at the junction of important roads bringing traffic in and out of the village. Commercial and public buildings were concentrated in this area. Morris, Cherry Valley, and many small hamlets are still oriented around a four corners with the main street crossing or extending from this intersection.

Each of the villages selected here for discussion has a special developmental pattern illustrated by the remaining building forms and environmental features. Other, smaller communities scattered throughout the twenty-four townships also have distinctive structural features which readers are encouraged to observe.

While landmark buildings are located throughout Otsego County, certain villages contain special groups of buildings termed "historic districts." These are definable geographic areas with high concentrations of intact structures of historical and architectural interest. The entire core of the village of Gilbertsville, for instance, is listed as a historic district on the National Register of Historic Places. Within larger towns are landmark neighborhoods, such as the Walnut Street Historic District in Oneonta, and the Main Street District in Worcester.

The importance of a historic district is not necessarily based on the value of the particular structures within its boundaries. The individual structures may not be outstanding. It is the entire grouping of structures, the blend of examples from different periods, the overall scale of the buildings, and their relative position within their surroundings which is important.

The historic districts in Otsego County range from the entire village of

Cooperstown, with its extraordinarily diverse resources, to the Walnut Street Historic District in Oneonta, a selective and integrated grouping of residential structures located within the larger city. The districts that have been defined up to the present do not constitute all the possible districts in the county; others which would certainly qualify lack only the necessary documentation.

Certain small villages, such as Burlington Flats, might qualify in their entirety. In other, larger communities such as Unadilla, Morris, Richfield Springs, and Cherry Valley, districts are feasible, for they all have sections which meet the criteria for a district designation: some structures of outstanding historic and/or architectural significance; a body of structures with representative stylistic characteristics which are on their original sites and which have undergone relatively little renovation; special environmental features which complement the grouping of buildings; and few if any modern intrusions. Pending official documentation and designation it is imperative that these areas be regarded as deserving of protection.

Beyond the confines of village settings are numerous individual landmark structures either isolated in the countryside or part of farmsteads or industrial sites. Rural buildings generally reflect variations in craftsmanship and the use of local materials, as well as the effects of settlement and economic change on the landscape. An emphasis on agricultural pursuits throughout the county is evident in the extent and diversity of agricultural structures. These range from early hillside farmsteads to large, turn-of-the-century dairy barns; the examples included here only suggest the kinds and scope of agricultural building forms. Other extant forms in the countryside include mill sites, churches, schoolhouses, and dwellings. A significant portion of rural landmarks are obsolete and/or abandoned, testimony to the decline in rural population and the necessity for rural revitalization through adaptive re-use.

3

THE LAKE REGION

AT THE NORTHERN EDGE OF OTSEGO COUNTY bordering on the Mohawk Valley is a four-township region dominated by the presence of two lakes: Canadarago Lake in the towns of Richfield, Exeter, and Otsego; and Otsego Lake along the eastern edge of the town of Otsego. The latter, well known as the source for the Susquehanna River and as the "Glimmerglass" setting for James Fenimore Cooper's *Leatherstocking Tales*, had a pivotal role in the settlement of the interior of New York State. Both lakes have contributed to the region's longstanding reputation as a scenic and healthful vacation area.

Historic buildings in the lake region illustrate the rich and diverse history of this part of the county. Among the landmarks are some of the earliest buildings in the county (plates 30 and 59), the most formal architectural achievement in the county (plate 29), the largest historic district in the county (the village of Cooperstown), and significant vernacular structures (plate 43). Wood has been the primary building material in this region, although there are several limestone buildings in Springfield Township (plate 33), and Exeter Township has a concentration of stone structures (plates 45 and 46).

Rural parts of the lake region reveal buildings of the Federal and Greek Revival styles, farmsteads which have remained relatively unchanged in appearance though their functional importance has declined. The small villages in the region, many of which were located on major transportation routes, share a preponderance of early nineteenth-century structures. The former self-sufficiency of these communities is suggested by the presence of large homes and the remnants of industrial buildings, often empty. Indeed, several hamlets in the region, such as Monticello, have been termed "ghost towns" due to the large numbers of buildings now abandoned which were once the scenes of extensive activity. Architectural remains in larger villages such as Fly Creek and Toddsville reflect their former importance as manufacturing centers (plate 48).

The two largest villages in the region, Richfield Springs and Cooperstown, contain structural reminders of late nineteenth-century growth. Both of these communities were affected by railroad activity which preceded and made possible the great increase in resort activities at the turn of the century. Throughout the region development has been increasingly concentrated in these two villages, with a significant decline resulting in the rural population. In visiting the lake region travelers are urged to seek out rural landmarks as well as to visit particular villages.

29. HYDE HALL, Glimmerglass State Park, East Lake Road, Town of Springfield.
Construction on Hyde Hall began in 1817, when George Hyde Clarke arrived in the United States from England to settle on land granted to his father George Clarke. Designed by the Greek Revival architect Philip Hooker, who was responsible for the Albany Academy and the Hamilton College Chapel, and completed in 1833, Hyde Hall is a rare example of an American classical building that derives from European forms.

Hyde Hall has the qualities of a great English manor house expressed in the way it is sited, dominating the lake, and in its relationship to all lesser buildings, separated as it is from the surrounding farms and dependencies by a bridge and gatehouse. The building itself is monumental, strong, almost devoid of ornament. The façade is severe, the usual number of windows has been reduced, the portico looms as would one of a bank or a mausoleum or some grand commercial building, not merely that of a country house.

The use of stone and the massive proportions make this building different from any other Greek Revival structure in Otsego County. Even the Otsego County Bank Building (plate 10) seems overwhelmed by contrast. Only the Rotch Mansion in Morris (plate 112) approaches Hyde Hall in grandeur and scale. In all respects it appears to be the seat of a great landed family rather than the rural home of an ordinary American citizen.

Town of Springfield

30. RESIDENCE, County Route 29A, Springfield Center. This building is known locally as one of the earliest in the Springfield area: the steeply pitched gable and plain styling would suggest a date in the late eighteenth or early nineteenth century.

31. CATLIN MEMORIAL LIBRARY, County Route 29A, Springfield Center.
This small library is a most interesting vernacular expression combining elements of both the Queen Anne and the Shingle styles with its "candle-snuffer" roof and shingle sheathing and wood trim.

32. ABBY COTES WINSOR SELECT SCHOOL FOR GIRLS, Route 20, East of East Springfield. By 1825 Otsego County boasted at least ten private academies for secondary education. The Winsor School, a well-known academy for boarders and day students, was housed in this Federal building. Note the fully developed front portico—an unusual survival.

33. Francis Carriage Works, Hinds Road, North of Junction with Route 20, Springfield. The production of wagons was important for the self-sufficient communities of the early nineteenth century. Built in the 1830s, this structure housed a carriage shop and later a cabinet shop. The use of limestone for construction indicates its local availability.

34. Italianate Residence, Route 20, Springfield. This mid-century home is immediately identifiable as Italianate by the heavy cornice and its curvilinear brackets, along with double arched windows and their bold moldings. The porch has paired colonettes and decorative woodwork. The symmetrical arrangement of the front façade is a variation on the Italian villa design.

Town of Richfield

35. CORN CRIB, Route 28, South of Richfield Springs. Included in the complex of outbuildings on the Baker Farm is this stone corn crib. In plan it is not unusual, but its execution in stone is atypical for Otsego County. The corn crib complements the large octagonal barn situated nearby (plate 21). In addition to barns and corn cribs, numerous other outbuildings such as smokehouses, granaries, and sugarhouses were essential elements of farming units in the county. These were all vernacular structures built with a sense of function, tradition, and local adaptation rather than exact design.

Village of Richfield Springs

Richfield Springs has always had an advantageous location situated just north of Canadarago Lake. The village grew up around the site of an ancient sulphur springs and since 1822 has benefited from popular interest in mineral water treatments. Located on the routes of the Skaneateles and the Great Western turnpikes, the village was accessible to travelers and settlers moving westward from Albany. Also on the route of the railroad which later linked Albany and Utica, it became a natural stopover for vacationers.

Village structures vividly recall these earlier developments. The Spring House Park and its bandstand, the large-scale commercial section which once housed prestigious hotels and businesses, and the skeletons of once-conspicuous boarding houses all indicate the village's former role as a substantial resort community. Most of these structures were built during the peak of the resort era, and while few of them are stylistically pure, they are fascinating eclectic variations on the styles which were in vogue in the 1880s and 1890s (plates 37 and 38). The extant buildings are simply the remnants of what was once a plentiful collection of large boarding homes; many of these were razed after the resort business dropped off in 1929. The subsequent decline in traffic and commerce has been partially compensated for by the village's location on Route 20, still a major east-west route connecting Albany and western New York.

36. **SPRING HOUSE PARK AND BANDSTAND, Main Street (Route 20), Richfield Springs.** The Spring House Park was first laid out in 1823, shortly after the discovery on the site of the sulphur springs, which were said to have value in the treatment of a variety of diseases and which were to attract vacationers in large numbers. The park has always been carefully kept up by residents. In 1857 the area was planted with numerous trees, and later a prominent summer visitor, Thomas R. Proctor of Utica, raised and landscaped part of the park. The village evolved so that residential structures were located to

the north of the park and commercial structures to the south. The well-preserved park area, with its blend of early and late nineteenth-century buildings and with its unspoiled natural features, helps explain the attraction of the village.

37. Stansfield Villa, 76 Main Street (Route 20), Richfield Springs.
A large-scale variation of the Second Empire style, this is one of the many Victorian structures in Richfield Springs with similar excrescences, brackets, and decorative cupolas, almost all of which were constructed as boarding houses in the late 1870s and early 1880s when the village was popular as a vacation spot.

38. GLADSTONE BUILDING, Main Street (Route 20), Richfield Springs.
A large portion of the extant commercial section in Richfield Springs dates from the time when resort activity was at its height, the 1880s and 1890s. Some of the most prominent hotels were on Main Street near the Spring House Park (plate 36). This carefully designed structure was once the Elk Hotel, advertised nationally as a convenient location for visiting the village known as the "Health Resort." The building has been successfully adapted for contemporary use, housing a variety of small businesses.

39. St. John's Episcopal Church, Main Street (Route 20), Richfield Springs.
One of the outstanding church buildings in the county, St. John's was constructed in 1880. The continuing use of the Gothic style for ecclesiastical structures is evident: here the style is executed in wood, with decorative work that would formerly have been carved in stone now rendered in wood. The retention of the original board and batten siding is a notable feature, as is the memorial window over the entrance designed by Tiffany and donated by the Proctor family of Utica who summered in Richfield Springs.

40. McGrath Funeral Home, James Street and Elm Street, Richfield Springs.
This former residence is an example of the Stick style which occurred in the 1870s and 1880s, along with other eclectic tendencies. It is unusual in its combination of stonework below and board and decorative wood siding above. Note the original iron fence with decorative heart motifs.

41. STABLE FOR MCCORMICK COTTAGE, Warren Street, Richfield Springs.
Numerous political and literary figures frequented Richfield Springs for its health cures in the late nineteenth century. Among them was industrialist Cyrus McCormick who had a large "cottage" constructed on Sunset Hill north of the village in 1882. The house was designed by the New York firm of McKim, Mead, and White and the grounds by Frederick Law Olmstead. The McCormick Cottage was razed in 1957, but the carriage house of similar design still stands. Note the stucco panels with inset pieces of colored glass from the workers' lunchtime beer bottles. The original chimneys have been removed.

Town of Exeter

42. RESIDENCE, South of Junction of Route 51 and Route 22, West Exeter.
This Greek Revival house, built in the 1830s, is one of the few remaining examples of cobblestone construction in the county.

43. STONE STORE, Junction of Angel Hill Road and Route 22, Exeter Center.
This stone structure built in 1829 was used continuously as a store and post office until relatively recently. With simple classical features, original windows and interior, and the typically rough ashlar stonework found in the western parts of the county, the building is a landmark which is both visually and historically significant.

44. CUMMINGS HOMESTEAD, Angel Hill Road, Exeter Center. One of the very few dwellings still occupied in a hamlet which has been virtually abandoned, this early (said to be eighteenth-century) residence has features typical of the period of early settlement: massive, deep plan; central chimney; rectangular small-paned windows; and simple doorway with detached sidelights.

46. HERKIMER HOUSE, Route 28, Schuyler Lake. This stone Greek Revival residence which dates from about 1840 is said to have been built by George Herkimer. The stonework is similar to that on the Old Stone Church (plate 45).

45. OLD STONE CHURCH, Junction of Route 28 and Route 22, Schuyler Lake.
The Old Stone Church was built in 1839–40 by George Herkimer, a nephew of Nicholas Herkimer. Long considered a local landmark, this is an unusual variation on the Greek Revival style. The steeple tower has been renovated several times, as has the interior. Various denominations use the structure which also houses the local historical society.

Town of Otsego

47. STONE MANSION, Route 28, Oaksville. The stone mansion was built for Rufus Steere, cotton merchant. Situated on a knoll overlooking the road, it has particularly striking stonework of variegated colors. The seeming disproportion between the heaviness of the pediment and the slimness of the high columns, as well as the crudely simple features suggest the local origin of the builder.

48. MILL, Oaksville. At one time there were seven large cotton mills in Otsego County. This one, built in 1830 and photographed here in 1894, is no longer standing but is important to illustrate the size and form of such structures. The building has simple classical lines typical of the Greek Revival period. This is similar to the mill in Index that was razed to provide the stone for Fenimore House (plate 73) in 1931.

49. Dairy Barn, Hoke Road, between Oaksville and Fly Creek. While the typical Otsego County barn does not emphasize appearance as much as function, the late nineteenth-century barns which were built to accommodate a growing dairy industry often had decorative cupolas and ornamental woodwork at the openings. This large barn has decorative trim as well as the large proportions typical of the 1870s and 1880s.

50. CIDER MILL, Goose Road, off County Route 26, North of Fly Creek.
The mill now known as the Old Cider Mill was built in 1856. It was operated as a cider mill from 1875 for many years, processing the fruit brought by farmers from the surrounding area. Now restored, the Old Cider Mill continues to serve area residents, with the original cast iron wheel still powered by water from the adjacent mill pond.

51. CARR HOMESTEAD, Front Entrance, Stone House Road, Northwest of Toddsville. This stone house must have been built in the early decades of the nineteenth century, for the characteristic herringbone pattern of the stonework is said to have been done by "Scotch Jamie," the Cooperstown builder mentioned in James Fenimore Cooper's *Wyandotte* who was also responsible for the Pomeroy Place in Cooperstown (plates 4 and 5). The porch is a later addition.

52. Cotton Mill, Route 28, Index. This is one of the few survivals from the era when seven large mill complexes were operating in Otsego County. This stone mill, part of the Hope Factory (now Index) was built for Squire Steere in 1815 (plate 47). It has served area farmers continuously. During the building of the Cooperstown and Susquehanna Valley Railroad it furnished teamsters' horses with feed.

Village of Cooperstown

Cooperstown is the best-known village in the county, drawing thousands of visitors each year to its museums and lakeside attractions. The village derives its special identity from a combination of elements, including diverse architectural features, strong historical and literary associations, and outstanding natural features. It is nationally known not only as the site of the Baseball Hall of Fame and the home of novelist James Fenimore Cooper, but also as one of the most scenic and best-preserved communities in the northeast.

The Cooperstown Historic District, listed on the National Register of Historic Places, encompasses the central, most historic core of the community as well as the outer fringes of the village with its later vernacular structures. There is a concentration of important landmarks in the district, including early churches, prominent residences, the landmarks associated with the Cooper family, and a notable commercial section.

Historically, Cooperstown has been one of the economic centers of the region, serving a wide surrounding area. This role was sustained and expanded during the railroad era. Twentieth-century influences on the village have brought significant changes. Cooperstown now functions primarily as a museum and tourist center. This role, fortunately, has helped in the maintenance and preservation of the village's historic structures. Any description of Cooperstown should contain reference to the various natural features and community amenities which contribute to its character: Otsego Lake, the parks, the monuments, and the landscaping. There are few villages in Upstate New York with the combination of structural, historic, and natural resources Cooperstown enjoys.

There are so many significant buildings in Cooperstown that this listing can only suggest the scope of the village's architectural heritage. The traveler is urged to explore on foot. A simple method of covering all the sites is to start at the junction of Chestnut and Main streets and branch out alternately in different

53. LAKELANDS, 8 Main Street, Cooperstown. During the first two decades of the nineteenth century prominent residents of the growing village constructed substantial homes which still today are remarkable for their proportions, siting, and design. One of these is Lakelands, built in 1802–1804 by Ira Steere and situated on spacious grounds overlooking the head of Otsego Lake. The solid mass of the building, the end-wall fireplaces, the simplicity of moldings, and the centered door with semicircular fanlight place the building in the Federal period.

directions, each time returning to the four corners. The reader is encouraged to examine the commercial section, one of the most varied and complete in the county, and the side streets with their many intact vernacular structures.

54. EDGEWATER, River Street and Lake Street, Cooperstown.
Another of Cooperstown's early mansions is this brick house constructed for Isaac Cooper, brother of James Fenimore Cooper, between 1810 and 1812. The brickwork is said to have cost $522. The house has been changed and added to over the years: the ballustrade was added during the mid-nineteenth century, and in 1920 architect Frank P. Whiting worked on the house. Set back from the street, the house commands a view of Otsego Lake beyond.

55. **TWIN HOUSES, 18 Main Street, Cooperstown.** Built in 1814, this well-preserved pair of houses is unusual for Otsego County. Superb examples of Federal architecture here executed in brick, they are, moreover, built as townhouses, a form rarely used in the county. They reflect the growing prosperity of the village in the early nineteenth century.

56. JOHNSTON-WOOD HOUSE, 48 River Street, Cooperstown. The slim silhouette of this home, the balanced five-bay façade, the arched doorway with sidelights, and the early twelve over twelve panes seem to confirm the 1810 construction date mentioned in village assessment records. Certainly this is one of the most intact examples of the late Georgian period to be found in the county.

57. **CHRIST CHURCH, 46 River Street, Cooperstown.** Built in 1807, this early Federal church was renovated in the Gothic style by James Fenimore Cooper in 1841. His comments on the changes, as noted by Ralph Birdsall in *Fenimore Cooper's Grave and Christ Churchyard*, expressed the sentiments of a generation that embraced the Gothic style as the most appropriate style for ecclesiastical buildings: "I have just been revolutionizing Christ Church, Cooperstown . . . converting its pine interior with oak — BONA FIDE oak. . . . It is really a pretty thing — pure Gothic, and is the wonder of the country round."

58. PRESBYTERIAN CHURCH, 69 Pioneer Street, Cooperstown. This was the first church in Cooperstown, built in 1805–1807 by twin brothers, Cyrus and Cyrenus Clark. The present steeple was added during renovations in 1887. The burial ground behind the church, like other early cemeteries in the county, contains interesting epitaphs. The land on which the church was built was donated by Judge Cooper.

59. OLD SMITHY, 55 Pioneer Street, Cooperstown. The smithy was built in 1786 by Judge William Cooper during the first year of settlement and is the oldest structure in the village. The interior of the first floor still has exposed the stump of a tree growing when the structure was built and which was used to support the blacksmith's anvil. The upper stories were added several years later, c. 1790. The Old Smithy is used as an art gallery during summer months.

60. IRONCLAD BUILDING, 92 Main Street, Cooperstown. As part of the general development of building technology in the mid-nineteenth century, the technique of casting in iron was applied successfully to buildings. Large sections could be cast and shipped more efficiently than had ever before been possible. Moldings and trims could be easily duplicated. During the 1860s and 1870s cast iron structures appeared in communities across the country, generally in the form of large commercial buildings. While fragments of cast iron buildings exist elsewhere in the county, the Ironclad Building is the major example of the technique in the area. Erected in 1862, this elaborate structure was ordered from the firm of James Bogardus of New York.

61. FIRST NATIONAL BANK BUILDING, 97–99 Main Street, Cooperstown.
During the late nineteenth century many local villages experienced devastating fires which destroyed whole sections of their main streets. Cooperstown was no exception. After the fire of 1862 a large section of Main Street was rebuilt with remarkable stylistic unity. The bank building was constructed in 1890–91 in the Romanesque style, using brick and stone and the characteristic heavy arches. Though a one-story addition was built early in the twentieth century, the character of the building is virtually unchanged.

62. STABLE, Chestnut Street, Cooperstown. It is not unusual to find examples in the county of utilitarian structures which express the building fashions of the times. The arched windows and decorated cupola of this stable place it in the third quarter of the nineteenth century.

63. Dow Funeral Home, 82 Chestnut Street, Cooperstown.
Only the pierced bargeboards remain to identify the Gothic origin of this extensively remodeled residence, now serving as a funeral home. Along Chestnut Street are other fine examples of mid-nineteenth century homes, particularly Italianate dwellings, some quite substantial.

64. WILLOWBROOK OR COOPER INN, 19 Chestnut Street, Cooperstown.
The Cooper Inn, an elegant structure executed in brick, was built in 1813–16. Since 1936 it has served as an inn where visitors to the village may admire its exceptional interior woodwork. The building was enlarged in the early twentieth century.

65. OTSEGO COUNTY JAIL, 195 Main Street, Cooperstown. The jailhouse at the county seat is one of the finest examples of Second Empire architecture in the county. Special features are the variations in window trim at each story, the steeply sloped mansard roof, interrupted by dormers, and the crowning cupola with bold moldings. The building currently serves as a jail and sheriff's headquarters. A recent additon at the rear does not overly detract from the original appearance.

67. DELAWARE AND HUDSON RAILROAD STATION, 204 Main Street, Cooperstown.
The elegant stone station was opened in 1916 and served the village until 1934. It is currently used as a residence. Note the herringbone stonework on the end wall and on the gable.

66. OTSEGO COUNTY COURTHOUSE, 193 Main Street, Cooperstown.
Syracuse architect Archimedes Russell designed this courthouse in 1880. Its design was not entirely satisfactory to the local legislators who had commissioned the work. As far as they were concerned it was "not beautiful to look at." Today, however, the intricate patterning and the interplay of triangular masses are exciting visual elements of the building.

68. Cooperstown and Charlotte Valley Railroad Station, Railroad Avenue, Cooperstown. The Cooperstown and Charlotte Valley Railroad was organized in 1865. The sixteen-mile line between Cooperstown and the Albany and Susquehanna Railroad at Cooperstown Junction was opened in 1869, the same year that this station was built.

69. 2, 4, 6 PINE BOULEVARD, Cooperstown. While Cooperstown is best known for its major historic landmarks, the attractive atmosphere of the village depends, too, on the number and variety of well-designed and well-maintained buildings spanning all periods of American architectural styles. The houses along Pine Boulevard form but one attractive residential grouping in the village. Most of the structures which line the street are modest vernacular buildings of the late nineteenth century. None of them is pure in the stylistic sense, and few of them have entirely escaped renovation over the years. However, they combine in such a way as to produce the impression of a substantial and pleasing residential grouping — certainly an important part of the Cooperstown environment.

70. **MCKIM HOUSE, 5 Westridge Road, Cooperstown.** Built in 1884, this is one of the best examples in the county of the Shingle style. Note the extension of the roof line to cover the entire house, the small windows, and the overall emphasis on horizontals. The house was part of a carefully designed complex, which included a Shingle style carriage house, by Babb, Cook, and Willard of New York.

71. **OTESAGA HOTEL, Lake Street, Cooperstown.** Cooperstown has long been a vacation and meeting spot, and the palatial Otesaga Hotel built by the Clark family in 1909 epitomizes this role. Its continuing use as a conference center and resort hotel affirms that the original natural and social attractions of the village for its early visitors still pertain today.

72. MASONIC HALL, 30 Lake Street, Cooperstown. The old Masonic Hall is one of the last remaining eighteenth-century structures in Cooperstown. It is the oldest Masonic Hall in the county and served in that capacity for more than sixty years. Built in 1797, the "raising, closing, glazing and completion" of the building cost £300. Despite several alterations, the five-bay sash, overall shape, and fine cornice detailing testify to its vernacular Georgian inception.

73. **NEW YORK STATE HISTORICAL ASSOCIATION, Lake Road, North of Cooperstown.** In 1931 Fenimore House was constructed of stone from nearby early cotton mills (plate 48) as a private home replacing the early nineteenth-century Fenimore House which had been the home of James Fenimore Cooper. The elegant Neo-Classical Revival style and magnified proportions are most appropriate to the building's imposing setting above the western edge of Otsego Lake. In 1948 the house and much of its valuable contents were given to the New York State Historical Association to be used as a headquarters and museum of American decorative arts. Since that time the structure has functioned effectively as the center of a growing museum and research complex.

Farmers' Museum and Village Crossroads

The Farmers' Museum and its Village Crossroads are located just north of Cooperstown on the west side of Otsego Lake. One of three museums maintained by the New York State Historical Association, the Farmers' Museum complex is a "living re-creation of life on the early New York frontier." The Village Crossroads is a grouping of representative village structures moved to the site to form an interpretive complex. Though not all the buildings are from Otsego County, they provide a special opportunity for visitors to observe and examine at close hand the structural details which are similar to other privately owned buildings in the area.

The seven Otsego County structures which are now part of the Village Crossroads are some of the most important in the complex. The buildings and their original locations are: Drug Store, from Hartwick (1832); Schoolhouse, from Filer's Corners (1828); Country Store, from Toddsville (1820); Printing Office, from Middlefield (1828); Doctor's Office, from Westford (1830s); Lawyer's Office, from Cooperstown (1829); and Lippitt Homestead (plate 2), from Hinman Hollow (1800).

While the Village Crossroads is a re-created grouping, the buildings have been carefully chosen as illustrative of their functions and time periods. They have been sited to blend logically with one another and sympathetically with the natural features of the museum setting. Each has historical significance which pertains as much in its present location as on its original site. Thus while the Village Crossroads cannot be defined as the typical historic district, it does have special significance as a rare grouping of architecturally and historically important local buildings.

74. VILLAGE CROSSROADS, Farmers' Museum, Cooperstown. The collection of buildings at the Farmers' Museum, the majority of them Otsego County structures, illustrates the variety and quality of vernacular building in this region.

75. Doctor's Office and Printing Office, Village Crossroads, Farmers' Museum, Cooperstown. The Printing Office, right, from Middlefield, and the Doctor's Office, left, from Westford, are similar to other buildings of traditional function and design still seen in the county (plate 202).

76. LOG BARN, Farmers' Museum Cooperstown. The only log structure still clearly visible in Otsego County, the log barn at the Farmers' Museum originated in neighboring Chenango County. Constructed with barked logs sheathed with hand-sawn hemlock boards, the barn is an important reminder of a traditional building technique now virtually extinct.

4

UPPER UNADILLA VALLEY

THE THREE TOWNSHIPS OF PLAINFIELD, EDMESTON, AND PITTSFIELD at the northwestern edge of Otsego County are most closely associated with the Unadilla River, which is the western boundary of the county, separating it from Chenango and Madison counties. Through the region runs a ridge of hills which divides it from the Butternut Creek Valley to the east and partially accounts for its relative isolation from the rest of the county.

The architectural features of the Upper Unadilla Valley reveal minimal development in the region since the mid-nineteenth century. Originally settled by scattered groups of New Englanders, with growth limited to those communities located near sources of water power, this region was relatively unaffected by the economic and demographic changes which occurred in other sections of the county.

The history of the entire region has been primarily agricultural, expressed in the scattered farmsteads which constitute the bulk of the extant structures. While no longer economic centers, small villages and hamlets continue to provide a focus for social concerns. Edmeston, the most important village in the region, is the one where later nineteenth-century development did occur—this due to the construction of the railroad (plate 85). Other villages, such as Pittsfield and Unadilla Forks (so named after the confluence of the two branches of the Unadilla River), have undergone few changes since the Greek Revival period. The structures in these hamlets are primarily rural versions of the Federal or Greek Revival styles. Outbuildings, constructed as needs dictated, often reflect later building fashions.

A distinctive feature of this region is the large residences built in the Victorian era. There are not many such homes—most of the farms retain their earlier homesteads — but several important examples can be found along the river corridor. With large proportions and exuberant details, these Victorian houses resemble others of the same period located just across the Unadilla River near the Chenango County village of New Berlin.

In traveling through the Upper Unadilla River region visitors will find that landmarks are widely scattered, but those that remain are delightfully original and intact examples.

Town of Plainfield

77. RESIDENCE, Route 18, between Route 20 and Unadilla Forks.
The proliferation of Italianate brackets at the eaves and the fanciful sawn wood trim on the porch make this mid-nineteenth century home a striking example of the originality of vernacular builders.

78, 79. RESIDENCE, Route 18, North of Junction with Route 18A, Unadilla Forks. In Unadilla Forks there are five houses said to have been erected around 1820 by two early builders, Henry Wilcox and Parley Phillips. This Federal residence has features common to all the houses, distinguishing them as the work of talented local craftsmen: a skillfully designed front façade, with well-proportioned Ionic pilasters, recessed arches, delicate molding details, and an elegant entranceway.

80. **WILLIAMS HOUSE, "Williams Corners," Junction of Route 18 and Route 19, Town of Plainfield.** This structure is an elaborate example of Italianate vernacular, with decidedly unique variation in tower shapes, the two-story entrance bay, and the bracketed window hood moldings. The Underwood brothers of Edmeston are thought to have built the house in 1889 (plate 87).

81. **WOODEN SILO, "Williams Corners," Junction of Route 18 and Route 19, Town of Plainfield.** Like other agricultural structures in Otsego County, silos are such common features of the landscape that their existence and their design are taken for granted. However, as more farms are either modernized and expanded or completely abandoned, once-common forms such as this wooden silo are becoming increasingly rare. This example is typical of the mid-nineteenth century and still functions effectively as part of a farming unit.

82. RESIDENCE, between Junction of Route 18 and Route 19 and the Unadilla River. Built in the 1880s, this large residence has the exuberant detailing characteristic of many of the elaborate Italianate dwellings located just across the Unadilla River in and near the Chenango County village of New Berlin. Note the original iron cresting on the roof of the cupola and the hooded window moldings.

Town and Village of Edmeston

83. "Five Sisters," Route 80, South of Junction with Route 20, Edmeston.
This five-unit apartment building, built in the Neo-Classical Revival style in the 1890s, was once a showplace in the village. The form is unusual: it is one of the earliest multiple dwellings in the area. Note the careful variation in window treatment.

84. Barber Shop, Main Street (Route 80), Edmeston. Even the smallest nineteenth-century commercial buildings reflected prevailing architectural fashions. On Main Street in Edmeston, where there are several larger commercial structures dating from the end of the century, this small and whimsical barber shop built in the 1880s stands out as an example of local craftsmanship. Working in the then-popular Stick style, the builder was able to create a rich variety of surface textures and motifs on a small façade.

85. RAILROAD YARDS, Edmeston. The once-active complex of structures which still stands along the rail lines in Edmeston reflects the role of the village during the railroad era. After the Wharton Valley region (covering most of the township of Edmeston) was linked with communities further west by the extension of the Wharton Valley Line to Edmeston in 1889, the Edmeston station and the surrounding feed and farm supply buildings were an important service center. The station is characteristic of the 1890s, with its projecting roof line and decorative Stick style woodwork. Unfortunately, it is fast falling into disrepair. The other utilitarian structures, simple and functional, still serve a variety of supply-related purposes.

86. SMOKEHOUSE, Gazlay Farm, Route 18, South of South Edmeston.
Jacob Gazlay settled on this site in 1820. The smokehouse which is part of the original homestead is notable for the herringbone pattern in its stonework.

Town of Pittsfield

87. RICHIED PLACE, Route 80 between Pittsfield and Edmeston.
Like so many vernacular buildings, this structure combines elements of more than one style: a mansard roof was added to the cupola of the Italianate form. The Underwood brothers of Edmeston, well-known local builders during the Victorian era (plate 80), are said to have constructed the house in 1899.

88. CHAPIN HOUSE, Route 80, Town of Pittsfield. This striking residence was constructed c. 1880 for John Chapin who, according to local tradition, wanted to have the finest house in the area. Here the extra Gothic tracery in the apex of the gables and over the windows suggests the skill of the local builder.

89. Residence, "Hoboken Corners," Junction of Route 80 and County Route 18, Town of Pittsfield. The external features of this residence near the western boundary of the county are well preserved and reflect both Federal and Greek Revival tendencies. The house is said to have been used at one time as the factory store for the Arkwright Cotton Mills which stood just south of Hoboken.

90. **BEARDSLEY HOP HOUSE, "Hoboken Corners," Junction of Route 80 and County Route 18, Town of Pittsfield.** Hop houses, easily distinguished by their steeply pitched roofs with ventilating caps, were the buildings in which hops were smoked or dried. Some were separate structures while some are still attached as sections of larger barn complexes. Hops, the basic ingredient of beer, were at one time a mainstay of the county's economy. Many hop houses have been relegated to use as storage sheds or allowed to deteriorate. The Beardsley farm was originally settled in 1799. The hop house still standing on the property is one of the few surviving examples in this part of the county. At one time nearly every farm between Edmeston and New Berlin had at least one hop house.

91. GOTHIC RESIDENCE, Route 13 between Morris and Pittsfield, Town of Pittsfield.
Despite years of neglect, this Gothic house retains its original features: vertical siding, pointed gables, and decorative bargeboard.

5

BUTTERNUT CREEK VALLEY

THE BUTTERNUT VALLEY REGION is one of the most scenic sections of Otsego County. Extending from the township of Burlington on the north to Butternuts on the south, the region follows the southwestern path of the Butternut Creek to its outlet at the Unadilla River. The name Butternuts is derived from three butternut trees growing from one stump which were a reference point for the division of three early patents incorporating much of the land in the region.

The buildings in the Butternut Valley complement the scenery at the same time that they reveal the patterns of historical development. In the southern part of the valley, settled quite early due to its proximity to the then-navigable Unadilla River, population has always been concentrated near the two principal villages of Gilbertsville and Morris. Here may be found the large homes of prosperous citizens, highly developed adaptations of most of the nineteenth-century building styles (plate 112). Their counterparts in modest versions are plentiful as well: homes of millworkers in Morris and craftsmen in Gilbertsville are still clearly evident (plate 116). The commercial sections which remain in these towns date from the late nineteenth century, both areas having been subject to severe fires in the 1880s and 1890s (plate 107).

Remnants of early industrial buildings can be found throughout the region. Mills and small industries were located along the length of the creek to take advantage of the power it provided. From Garrattsville, through New Lisbon, to Gilbertsville, mill sites abound (plate 94).

In the northern sections of the region, population was scarcer and buildings, as a consequence, fewer in number. The farmsteads and isolated hamlets located above the creek valley reveal the popularity of Greek forms at the time when the area was growing. These sections have been virtually untouched by economic change since the Greek Revival period: late nineteenth- and early twentieth-century buildings are rare.

In the Butternut Creek Valley region, as in other sections of Otsego County the hamlets and villages are conspicuous for their historic qualities. Often without conscious preservation efforts, residents have been concerned to retain those features of their own landscape which were familiar to them. Readers are urged to travel throughout the region, sampling its varied natural and structural resources while considering the benefits of creating long-term protection for them.

Town of Burlington

93. **STONE MEETINGHOUSE, Route 51, Burlington Flats.** The stone residence on the green was built by one of the Wallbridge brothers, settlers from Connecticut who were instrumental in developing the community on Wharton Creek. It is said to have been the site of church meetings as early as 1801. Construction details would confirm an early date: simple plan, rough fieldstone walls, and arched fanlight.

92. **VILLAGE GREEN, Route 51, Burlington Flats.** The vista across the village green in Burlington Flats is one which is repeated, with variations, in other villages in the county. The structural elements of the scene — a classical Presbyterian Church, center, with its original sheds, a schoolhouse, left, and an early homestead, right — combine with such other elements as the cemetery and the open green to convey a vivid impression of rural village life. There are few settings in Otsego or in neighboring counties as intact as this one.

94. WALLBRIDGE MILL, off Route 51, Burlington Flats. Mill buildings were critical for the first settlers in Otsego County for grain, corn, and lumber. The need for gristmills and sawmills provides the most obvious clue as to the location of so many settlements near streams and creeks; without water power few communities could survive. By 1825 there were at least 125 gristmills in Otsego County. This is the only remaining evidence of an early mill complex (sawmill, gristmill, tannery, distillery) built by the Wallbridge brothers on Wharton Creek in the first years of the nineteenth century. Now used for storage, the large structure has twelve over twelve windows and classical moldings suggesting a construction date of c. 1820.

95. **CHURCH, Junction of Route 80 and Route 51, West Burlington.** After the Greek Revival period the Gothic became widely accepted as the appropriate style for ecclesiastical architecture. Even up to the present day the pointed arches, narrow windows, and vaulted ceilings of the Gothic style connote religious usage. The beautifully intact church in West Burlington is an outstanding example of vernacular craftsmanship.

Town of New Lisbon

96. ELNATHAN NOBLE HOUSE, Morris Town Line Road, near Junction with Route 12, New Lisbon. New Lisbon was originally named Noblesville after the Noble family who settled here in 1797. A superb example of the Greek Revival style, this house was built for Elnathan Noble in the early 1830s. The ballustrade at the roof line is unusual for Otsego County and is a stylistic carry-over from the earlier Federal period.

97. First Congregational Church, New Lisbon. First built in 1819–20, this church was renovated in 1870. Unfortunately, the building has been abandoned for church use and is falling into disrepair. Like other Greek Revival churches of the early nineteenth century in the county, this one has a simplified meetinghouse plan, with a square tower and pediment supported by four multisided columns.

98. Martin Noble House, Morris Town Line Road, near Junction with Route 12, New Lisbon. Martin Noble settled in Noblesville in 1797, and soon thereafter constructed this home. It was subsequently used for circuit court and as headquarters for the Meridian Sun Lodge. The house has simplified Federal features: symmetrical proportions, centered end-wall chimneys, and an unusually vernacular modification of the Palladian window.

99. MARTIN NOBLE CABINET SHOP, Junction of Route 41 and Route 12, New Lisbon. Martin Noble was a carpenter and joiner whose original shop building, known as "Major Noble's Cabinet Shop," has been subsequently used for a variety of commercial and crafts activities. The simple classical entablature and moldings framing the main opening are typical of the small crafts buildings which were once plentiful in Otsego County villages.

100. BARN, Route 14, between Lena and Welcome. Until the late nineteenth century decorative details were not often added to agricultural structures. This outbuilding, similar in shape to others of its kind, is made special by the addition of simple details. It still functions effectively as part of a farm complex. Note the original vertical siding.

101. OCTAGONAL BARN, Route 16, South of Garrattsville. One of two surviving octagonal barns in Otsego County (plate 21), this structure is still used as the central element of a working farm. Built in 1885, it has lost some original features but is worthy of preservation as a most unusual form of barn construction.

Town of Morris

102. NELSON LEWIS WAGON SHOP, Route 18, South New Berlin. Many of the structures associated with local production have disappeared, either through deterioration, fire, or neglect. This well-preserved wagon and woodworking shop, probably constructed in the 1830s and home of a thriving business run by the Lewis family for more than 100 years, is a special example of the type of functional structure, with slight stylistic embellishment, which housed important preindustrial activities. Note the dentils under the eaves and entranceway.

103. MORRIS MANOR, Route 51, between Morris and Gilbertsville, Town of Butternuts. One of the few manor houses in the area, this is the family seat for the Morris family, influential in the Butternut Valley for generations. The original portion of the house was constructed in 1805; the porch and other additions were made at the turn of the century. General Jacob Morris, son of Lewis Morris, a signer of the Declaration of Independence, received with his brother Richard a grant of thirty-three thousand acres in the Butternut Valley as indemnity for loss of property destroyed by the British during the American Revolution. The ravine and knoll next to Morris Manor form a scene in James Fenimore Cooper's *Wyandotte*.

104. **Morris Manor Chapel, Route 51 between Morris and Gilbertsville, Town of Butternuts.** "All Saints Chapel" was erected in 1870 as a private chapel by James Morris, grandson of General Jacob Morris. It is set in a beautifully landscaped park. An outstanding example of vernacular Gothic ecclesiastical architecture, the chapel is still used for family services.

Village of Morris

The hamlet of Louisville was founded approximately 1797, primarily by French émigrés. The village was later renamed Morris after General Jacob Morris, an early settler from New Jersey who contributed considerably to the development of the area.

Like so many other villages in Otsego County, Morris was once a large and bustling community, a service and transportation center for its immediate region. Large homes in the Federal, Greek Revival, or Italianate style; small, preindustrial buildings; an abandoned mill; churches from the early and mid-century; and a commercial district with mid- and late nineteenth-century sections — all these extant structures record growth and change in the village during the nineteenth century. There are virtually no twentieth-century structures, typical of Otsego County villages in which commerce and growth slowed after 1900.

A special feature of the village's architecture is the extensive use of stone. Local tradition maintains that Captain Dan Smith, a builder whose own home is located just south of the village, was responsible for many of the stone buildings, both residential and commercial structures.

Morris has enjoyed enough continuing prosperity to maintain a strong identity and sense of self-preservation. The village is an important stop for any traveler exploring the scenic Butternut Valley region.

105. VAN RENSSELAER HOUSE, Main Street (Route 51), Morris. A major landmark from the period of early settlement, this formal house harkens back to the earlier Georgian period—symmetrical plan, hipped roof, and classically simple cornice—while it exhibits obviously Federal detailing—arched fanlight over the central entry and sidelights, Palladian windows, and end-wall fireplaces. The house was built in 1814 for Colonel Volkert Van Rensselaer, at a time when the village of Morris consisted of but fourteen houses. It has an imposing location on landscaped grounds overlooking Butternut Creek.

106. ZION EPISCOPAL CHURCH, East Main Street, Morris. Erected in 1818–19 on land given by General Jacob Morris, this church was supported by such important local persons as the General, Judge Pascal Franchot, and Jacob Van Rensselaer. It was enlarged and extensively renovated in 1869, with the interior newly furnished, side galleries moved, the old windows replaced with stained glass, and a large recessed chancel added.

107. 6–14 WEST MAIN STREET, Morris. Along the west side of Main Street in Morris is a row of late nineteenth-century commercial buildings which provides a glimpse of village commercial activity at that time. While the two brick structures originally had fanciful projections and finials decorating the roof line, their lower stories are intact, unusual for commercial buildings. The sameness of scale, the continuity of design, and the harmonious relationship of the buildings to one another make this row an important grouping.

108. BUTTERNUT VALLEY ARTS AND CRAFTS BUILDING, 19 West Main Street, Morris.
On the east side of Main Street stands this late nineteenth-century commercial building with remarkably intact façade, in this instance a "boomtown front," so called because of the sense of height created by applying a three-story facing to a two-story structure. The original arrangement of street-level shop windows, the row of simple triangular pediments at the second stage, and the richly decorated roof line broken by a decorative central arch crowning a modified Palladian window are all evidence of an imaginative local craftsman working in the Stick style.

110. Butter Paddle Factory, 15 Grove Street, Morris. The largely self-sufficient communities of the early nineteenth century depended almost entirely on locally produced goods. The variety of local products which were made in Otsego County villages, some quite early, is amazing. Among other things Morris produced chairs, tobacco boxes, ink stands, and in this building butter paddles. The building has been remodeled; the early ten over ten panes in the windows (ten over ten on the side and twelve over twelve on the front) probably originated in a residence but, as was commonly done, were re-used in this outbuilding.

109. Firehouse, 27 West Main Street, Morris. Since 1880 the firehouse in Morris has served its original purpose. In recent years some of the ornamentation has been removed and aluminum siding applied. The cupola and window moldings are intact, however, and the picturesque quality of this important village building remains.

111. DAVIS-LULL HOUSE, North Broad Street and Maple Street, Morris.
Originally built for Jonathan Davis who owned vast tracts of land in the western part of the township, the house has been in the Lull family for some time. It sits on a knoll overlooking the village of Morris with wide views across the Butternut Valley. This is one of the best examples of Gothic construction in the county, and fortunately most of its original features have been preserved—the vertical board and batten siding, the drip hood molding on the windows, the umbrage (entry porch) with its octagonal columns, and the pointed arch of the front door. There is Gothic bargeboard trim on one of the barns as well.

112. **"The Grove," off Route 51, Morris.** "The Grove," a superb expression of Greek Revival style, is one of the outstanding features of Otsego County. The house and its grounds constitute a remarkably complete unit which conveys the life style of a mid-nineteenth-century gentleman farmer. Built in 1833–34, "The Grove" was for many years the home of Francis Rotch, a state senator and agricultural expert. There is some evidence that the builder was Captain Dan Mason, who is known to have done other, similar stone structures in the immediate vicinity. To the rear of the square, two-story main house is a frame extension of smaller scale. There are several outbuildings on the landscaped site including a unique wood frame gatehouse with delicate Federal trim.

Town of Butternuts

113. SOLON BENEDICT HOUSE, Lobdell Road, East of Gilbertsville.
The Benedict House is reputed to be both the oldest house in Butternuts and an original log cabin. Although the windows have been changed and a porch and wing added, it still retains the saltbox shape characteristic of the earliest dwellings.

114. RESIDENCE, Route 18, North of Mount Upton. This small residence built about 1815 is located adjacent to the Unadilla River, a transportation route in the early nineteenth century. This is obviously a country or vernacular version of the formal Federal style. The stonework is similar to other buildings at the western edge of the county—an unusual feature is the use of large irregular stone lintels over the windows.

Village of Gilbertsville

The village of Gilbertsville, located near the southern end of the Butternut Creek Valley, has long been recognized for its unspoiled residential qualities and its well-protected environmental features. Only relatively recently, however, has the village begun to receive deserved recognition for its unique architectural qualities. Not only does it contain a large historic district, with both formal and vernacular versions of most of the major American building styles, but it also contains a high proportion of major structures designed by prominent American architects. It is a rare occurrence that so many designed buildings as appear here would have been erected in such a remote rural area, far from any urban centers.

There are numerous reasons for the special architectural qualities of this village: the early prosperity of the first settlers, including Abijah Gilbert; success of local enterprises at the beginning of the nineteenth century and the shift to a successful role as a summer resort area at the end of the century; the strength of family and community ties which have persisted over generations; and the wealth and status of both residents and visitors throughout the history of the village.

Landmark structures abound in Gilbertsville. Many of them are located within the boundaries of the Gilbertsville Historic District, an area which includes the entire central portion of Gilbertsville and which is listed on the National Register of Historic Places. Documentation of the remainder of the village has been recently completed and is pending approval as an enlarged historic district. Within the original district there is a wide range of architectural forms, from simple Federal homes to late Greek Revival commercial structures, and including the unusual Major's Inn done in a Neo-Tudor style (plate 121).

Beyond the boundaries of the historic district are other landmarks, several of them significant architectural achievements by well-known designers. While they may incorporate early homesteads, or parts thereof, most date from the late nineteenth century and early twentieth century when successful village sons and summer visitors were desirous of constructing small estates which would properly reflect their status. One of these was Tianderah, designed by Boston architect William Ralph Emerson. An imposing amalgam of Romanesque and Shingle style elements, the mansion is dramatically situated overlooking the village of Gilbertsville and is surrounded by a formally designed park (plates 123 and 124).

To fully appreciate the various features of the village travelers should explore on foot. In doing so careful attention should be given to the ways in which different structures contrast with and complement one another, creating the special blend that gives Gilbertsville its distinctive visual character.

116. **3, 5 Spring Street, Gilbertsville Historic District, Gilbertsville.**
    While Gilbertsville is best known for its major landmarks, the more modest structures, carefully maintained and attractively situated in relation to one another, are in no small measure responsible for the atmosphere of the village. Such scenes as this one, including two vernacular structures—an Italianate building, left, and a Greek Revival home, right—surrounded by large trees and lawns, contribute to the overall architectural environment.

115. **Grange Hall (formerly the Presbyterian Church), 9 Bloom Street, Gilbertsville Historic District, Gilbertsville.** The Presbyterian Church, which combines a striking Georgian tower, Gothic windows, and classical pilasters, is one of the outstanding architectural features of the village, a major Gilbertsville landmark. It was built in 1832–33 but since 1884 has served as a village hall, town hall, and most recently as a grange hall. The restoration of its steeple was the focus of a Bicentennial project, resulting in replacement of the original with an exact replica. There is evidence to suggest that the builders of this church, the Rockwell brothers, also did the very similar Otego Presbyterian Church (plate 172). The pilasters on the façade and corners, the Greek fret ornament under the cornice of the pediments, and the beautifully molded tower and belfry would seem to have been done by the same builder.

117. Gilbertsville Free Library, 19 Commercial Street, Gilbertsville Historic District, Gilbertsville. The Gilbertsville Library has served the community in a variety of capacities, starting in 1818 as a schoolhouse, later as a blacksmith shop, and in 1888 remodeled to become the first free library in the county. It currently houses much important material relating to the history of the village and township.

118. **GILBERT BLOCK, 3, 6, 9 Commercial Street, Gilbertsville Historic District, Gilbertsville.** Designed by Henry F. Bigelow of Boston, this unusual commercial block expresses the interest in period revivals which occurred near the end of the nineteenth century. This block was constructed in 1893–95 to replace earlier commercial buildings destroyed by fire. The applied wooden strips are reminiscent of half-timbered structures in Tudor England. The free use of various decorative motifs is characteristic of vernacular buildings of the late nineteenth century. The Gilbert Block complements the impressive Major's Inn across the street (plate 121).

119. **GILBERTSVILLE POST OFFICE, 1 Commercial Street, Gilbertsville Historic District, Gilbertsville.** Set in the center of the Gilbertsville Historic District is one of the focal points of community life, the post office. The building originally had a false front; it was remodeled with modest classical features toward the end of the century. It exemplifies the effectiveness of continued usage of a historic structure for its originally intended function. The interior of the post office, with decorative Victorian features, is still perfectly intact. The post office is part of a small village park, one of several in the community.

120. **PRESBYTERIAN CHURCH, 19 Marion Avenue, Gilbertsville Historic District, Gilbertsville.** Erected in 1882–84, this is one of the finest examples in the county of Romanesque style ecclesiastical building with its rough-cut stonework, the round-arched windows, and the crenelated tower.

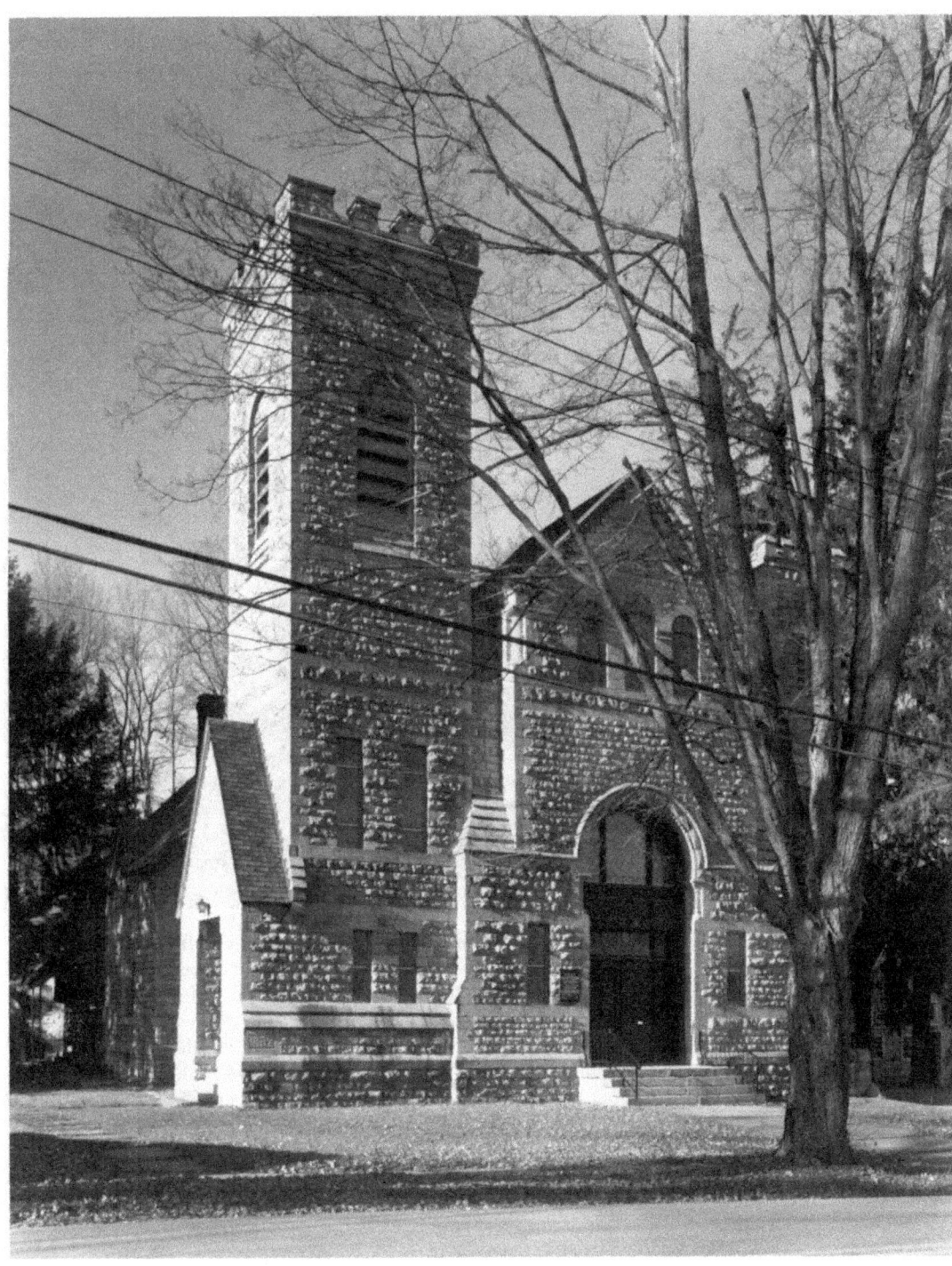

121. Major's Inn, Marion Avenue and Commercial Street, Gilbertsville Historic District, Gilbertsville. The original Gilbert Homestead which had stood on this site burned in 1895. Major James L. Gilbert then commissioned Augustus Nicholas Allen to construct the Inn, one of the best-known landmarks in the county. It reveals a very unusual blend of late nineteenth-century fascinations: medieval England, Gothic forms, and the interplay of different materials. The structure, one of the highlights of the historic district, has been put to a variety of uses, most recently as a summer theatre.

122. GILBERTSVILLE ACADEMY AND COLLEGIATE INSTITUTE, 1 Cliff Street, Gilbertsville Historic District, Gilbertsville. Built in 1839, the stone academy, left, was to become one of the best-known educational institutions in the state. It continued until 1896, when it was absorbed into the public school system. The present structure is *an enlargement of the original building. Unoccupied until recently, the Gilbertsville* Arts Center is now using the building for classroom and exhibition space. It is situated above the "Overlook," a village park developed in 1907 by Joseph T. Gilbert. The "Overlook" was constructed on the site of the Stag's Head Inn, a resort which burned in 1895. From the upper level of the grounds is an impressive view of the village and the Butternut Valley.

123, 124. TIANDERAH, off Spring Street, Town of Butternuts. William Ralph Emerson, a well-known New England architect, designed Tianderah, a rare instance of his work in so remote a location. Tianderah, left, is Romanesque or Richardsonian. The round-arched spandrel panels, the round entry arch, and the steep-pitched gables are all suggestive of the style, here executed as a regional variation in stone. The building's design is enhanced by its spacious landscaped setting above the village of Gilbertsville. The carefully designed stable, above, expresses the architect's facility with the Shingle style, also popular at the time.

6

UPPER SUSQUEHANNA RIVER BASIN

THE UPPER SUSQUEHANNA RIVER BASIN is a large, six-township region extending from the south end of Otsego Lake at the north to the confluence of the Susquehanna and Unadilla rivers at the south. The region takes its name from the Susquehanna River, which has undoubtedly been the single most important physical feature of Otsego County to influence development in the area. Much of the earliest exploration of the interior of New York State was made via the Susquehanna River. It was through this river valley that Revolutionary forces under General James Clinton and General John Sullivan passed in 1779 during their famous expedition to secure the southern New York and Pennsylvania borders.

    The Susquehanna River flows southwest from its source at Otsego Lake cutting a wide valley through the foothills of the Upper Catskill Mountains. The region incorporates these foothills, ridged sections dissected by creeks which drain into the valley. One of these, Otego Creek, creates a smaller valley extending from Hartwick through Laurens, to the point where it joins the Susquehanna River at Otego.

    The Upper Susquehanna River Basin includes landmark structures from all periods and all styles. Very early landmarks may be found (plate 129) as well as twentieth-century landmarks (plate 158). Formally designed buildings, although few in number, coexist with numerous vernacular structures. Within the region there is one officially recognized historic district on the National Register of Historic Places, the Walnut Street Historic District in Oneonta. There are several other districts and individual landmarks in the region which, when thoroughly documented, would probably meet the criteria for official listing.

The Upper Susquehanna River Basin clearly shows a shift from a rural to an urban economy, from a dispersed population to a more concentrated population base. Such a shift is obvious from the kinds of buildings which remain in certain parts of the region. While the northern areas and the hilly sections beyond the river basin were unchanged by the railroad, the communities located along its route were permanently changed, more so than in any other part of the county. Up to that time the region was similar in most respects to the rest of the county: small villages were self-sustaining economic units in which production and trade grew rapidly from 1800 to 1850. Village buildings from this time are Federal or Greek Revival, some of them pretentious homes or businesses (plate 133). Villages such as Hartwick and Otego still have the special mix of residences and public and commercial buildings which record their prosperity before decline took over in mid-century.

Agriculture also followed a typical pattern: diversification in the early years of the nineteenth century followed by a concentration on dairy or hops farming (or both). Rural structures in the contemporary landcape, many of which are still in use, reveal these changes. Whether farmsteads (plate 150) or hop houses (plate 126), they are as important for an understanding of historic and architectural change in the region as are other forms.

Significant manufacturing activity took place in the region in the first part of the century. Mills and cottage industries flourished, taking advantage of the power furnished by the river and its many tributaries. One of the largest textile mills in the county was located in the village of Laurens, the Otsego Cotton Mill. While few original industrial buildings survive, the homes of the managers and workers illustrate their impact (plate 137).

With the construction of the railroad through the valley in the 1860s, the vast transfer of population from county to town began. Commerce and transportation became increasingly concentrated in the villages along the river, with the result that outlying communities gradually relinquished their former roles as marketing centers and became residential communities in which little development occurred in the last 100 years. This decline in rural activity is clear in the small number of late nineteenth-century structures in the villages and countryside beyond the river valley. The rapid expansion and economic success of the towns along the route of the railroad are clearly reflected in the large numbers of substantial homes built in the Queen Anne and other Victorian styles, and the large-scale commercial structures with late nineteenth-century detailing (plate 156).

As a third phase in its development, the Upper Susquehanna Region is undergoing changes in the twentieth century brought about by the construction of the new highway, Interstate-88. Growth is concentrated along the route of this road, which runs parallel to the river and provides access to the various villages along the valley. These developments may be doubly beneficial to the region: while stimulating economic activity in the valley, the rerouting of traffic out of the villages may, in fact, act to preserve their architectural qualities.

Ranging from the smallest commercial structure (plate 133) to the largest public buildings (plate 158), the architecture of the Upper Susquehanna River Basin records the successive stages of growth and change more graphically than any other form of documentation. Travelers are urged to spend considerable time exploring this region, both the river valley towns and the adjacent rural areas.

Town of Hartwick

125. DR. GREENOUGH HOUSE, Junction of Greenough Road and Route 11, West of Index. This prominent Greek Revival residence varies from the usual porticoed house form. Rather than a two-story central block with a projecting pediment and flanking one-story wings, this house consists of a long one-and-one-half-story block with projecting center pediment. The qualities of strength and solidity usually conveyed by the Greek Revival style are somehow reinforced with this plan. Like several other landmarks, this house is supposed to have been a stop on the Underground Railroad.

126. Hop House, Route 59, between Toddsville and Route 11, Town of Hartwick.
Hops were at one time the most important industry in Otsego County. The last evidence of that era is the hop barns which dot the landscape. This one has the characteristic high roof, allowing for extra room to dry the vines.

127. SCHOOLHOUSE, Junction of Route 59 and Perkins Road, Town of Hartwick. District school buildings were mandatory by 1812; each township was divided into districts, and each district was responsible for erecting and maintaining its schools. The large rural population necessitated numerous schools. Since the decline of rural areas, consolidation of districts, and a diminishing rural population, many of these buildings have become obsolete. The first schools were similar to the first dwellings, crude and functional—a simple frame, wooden benches, and a chimney and stove. A woodshed and outhouse completed the complex. Throughout much of the nineteenth century and even in some areas into the twentieth century, these modest one-room schools served effectively. This small district school is typical: the simply framed door with headlight, the original panes which are nine over nine, the slim return of the eaves, and the small proportions. It is one of the few surviving examples of the earliest school buildings.

128. Cook Homestead, Petkewec Road, North of County Route 11, Town of Hartwick. In 1794 George Pearse settled here and erected a log cabin. In 1805 the cabin was replaced by this large tavern with its central chimney, large, symmetrical proportions, and steeply pitched roof. Many original features are intact, including the tavern bar. The house now functions as the office for a camping facility.

129. WHITE HOUSE OR BUTTERFIELD TAVERN, Route 205, North of Hartwick.
In 1786 Major James Butterfield purchased lands in Hartwick Township from Judge William Cooper of Cooperstown. Butterfield Tavern was built in 1792. A striking and substantial structure, it is said to have been one of the first buildings painted white in the country west of Albany. Strictly symmetrical proportions, large interior chimneys, narrow windows, keystone decoration on the lintels, and carved oval and dentilled pediment above the entrance are vernacular renditions of a Georgian transition to the Federal style.

130. WHITE HOUSE, Detail. An early family graveyard with this headstone commemorating Major Butterfield lies just south of the White House.

131. HOLDEN INN, Maples Road near Junction with Chase Road, Town of Hartwick. In 1794 Stephen Holden arrived in the town of Hartwick with only $120. Within ten years he had cleared a large piece of land and built the well-known tavern which still stands today. The first town meeting in the township was held there in 1804. Travelers going westward through the county regularly stopped here. Now a residence, the Holden Inn has a plan and details characteristic of the first large frame dwellings. Its massive central chimney is intact.

132. MAPLES HOMESTEAD, Maple Road, Town of Hartwick. David and Louise Maples emigrated from Connecticut to Hartwick Township in 1799 and settled on a parcel of land on the hills west of the Susquehanna River near the very center of Otsego County. This structure, the second on the site, has the substantial proportions and simplified details of the Greek Revival period. The house was enlarged as needs dictated: a rear wing accommodated the many hops pickers who worked on the site near the turn of the century when this and many other Otsego County farms were producing the largest crop of hops in the country. The Maples property, still in the possession of Maples descendants, contains a family cemetery and the site of the schoolhouse built for the Maples children in 1855.

133. BRESEE STORE, Junction of Route 11 and Route 11D, South Hartwick.
The first commercial buildings had much the same forms as early residential buildings: simple proportions, simplified classical details, and plain moldings around the openings. This early (c. 1810) commercial structure served for many years as a general store in the hamlet of South Hartwick. The building has retained many original features. About 1890 Frank Bresee started a store in the building, the beginning of a long business career leading to the establishment of Bresee's Department Store in Oneonta.

134. Proctor Place, Junction of Route 11 and Route 205, Hartwick.
The stone mansion at the four corners in Hartwick was built in 1833 by Dr. Freeborn D. Thrall, Hartwick's first physician. The brick building which he used for an office, and which stood near this structure, is now the Drug Store in the Village Crossroads of the Farmers' Museum in Cooperstown. The Proctor Place is rectangular, with a handsome row of six Ionic columns across the front supporting a one-story porch. The moldings and solid proportions are clearly Greek Revival.

135. BAPTIST CHURCH, Junction of Route 11 and Route 205, Hartwick.
Built in 1854, this structure shows a Greek Revival entablature and dentilling on the cornice and pediment. However, evidences of later styles appear in the window shapes and decorative scroll work. The two front doors date back to the eighteenth-century meetinghouse plan.

136. RESIDENCE, 303 East Main Street, Hartwick. The Queen Anne details on this 1880s residence reveal the emphasis during that period on textured surfaces, steeply pitched gables and extra dormers, and elaborate wood trim, particularly adorning porches. This home has been well kept and has retained its original trim.

Town and Village of Laurens

137. MAIN STREET, Laurens. Most of the historic structures which have survived in Laurens date from before 1850. There are few industrial buildings—what have survived are the homes of the early entrepreneurs, businessmen, and craftsmen. Erected mainly in the 1820s and 1830s, they all emphasize variations on classical treatments. While the two illustrated here have experienced some modernization, they suggest the early prosperity of the village and the former elegance of Main Street. The house at right was built for W. C. Fields, founder of the Otsego Cotton Mill; the other structure was the home of a businessman, William Comstock. Recent research indicates that Isaac Powell, a local builder, may have been responsible for many local homes including these two (plate 140).

138. GARDNER HOUSE, Route 11, South of Laurens. Built in 1818, this simple farmstead has the deep plan, steeply pitched gable, and symmetrical window placement characteristic of vernacular structures built during the period of early settlement. The simply embellished doorway and the half-round gable window suggest also an awareness of the Federal style. Although the exterior remains intact, the building's interior has been extensively altered.

139. RESIDENCE, Route 11A, North of Junction with Route 205, Town of Laurens.
A picturesque cottage, this transitional vernacular structure combines Greek Revival frieze windows and decorative board and batten siding, characteristic of the Gothic Revival, with molding suggestive of the later Italianate period.

140. MAYALL-POWELL HOUSE, Route 205, North of Laurens. Local builder Isaac Powell was responsible for numerous houses, churches, and barns in the central part of the county. His particular method of "four-square construction," exemplified here in his own house, was well known locally. The large house, constructed in 1818, has plain exterior features, squarish plan, and steep hipped roof typical of the earlier Georgian period. The interior, however, has remarkably carved Federal details. The construction is unusual in that the hipped roof is supported by a massive post ten inches in diameter with supports radiating up from it to the angles of the roof. The house is on the site of the first settlement in Laurens, made by Joseph Mayall.

141. **ARMSTRONG-STOCKING HOUSE, Detail, Route 205, between Laurens and Mount Vision.** Within the basic format of Greek Revival design much ornamental variation could occur. This elaborately worked gable end reveals the inventive spirit of an anonymous builder who had otherwise produced a substantial Greek Revival dwelling with typical classical elements. Local tradition reveals that so much expense was incurred in doing the exterior of the house that the owners could not afford to complete the interior.

142. WELLHOUSE, Route 205, Mount Vision. A seemingly insignificant outbuilding, this wellhouse is important as an intact example of a now-vanishing structural form. Note the mid-century details — projecting cornice and trim characteristic of the Italianate style.

143. **GREEK REVIVAL DWELLINGS, Route 205, Mount Vision.** There are few pairs of houses of any period in this state, and no others are known to survive in the county. These residences were built c. 1832 by two brothers and at one time were enclosed in a single fence of Greek Revival design. The houses were once nearly identical: a side wing was added to the house on the right sometime during the 1840s. The two houses exemplify the Greek Revival as it was expressed locally and throughout Central New York. The three front bays articulated by four columns, the use of the Doric order, the repeating tiers of dentils in the heavy pediment, the basic temple shape — all are features seen repeatedly in villages and rural locations in this area. Note the use of flush-boards, a device used to convey the impression of stonework, as siding on the house at the left.

144. OTEGO VALLEY GRANGE, Junction of Route 205 and Route 11B, Mount Vision. Originally the Jacksonville Hotel, this large structure has served as a focal point of community life since its construction in 1825. Used as a tavern through the 1930s, it is presently headquarters for the local grange and meeting place for other local organizations. Original features which survive are the long shape, the window and door placement, and some early glass. The portico, supported by octagonal columns, and some of the entrance moldings date from the Greek Revival era. Although the building is a hybrid stylistically, it nevertheless is significant as an example of a nineteenth-century tavern and as a continuous site for local activities.

145. SAYRE HOUSE, Route 28, Milford. Built in 1810 by David Sayre, an early settler from Greene County, this dwelling is a vernacular expression of the Federal style. The homestead is being restored by the Greater Milford Historical Society for use as a museum of local history.

Town of Milford

146. MILFORD NATIONAL BANK, East of Junction of Route 44 and Route 28, Milford. Many public buildings constructed in the early twentieth century were designed with classical elements and proportions; hence the term Neo-Classical Revival. The Georgian style doorway is reminiscent of ones found on frame houses in Connecticut two centuries earlier.

147. CULLEY TAVERN, Route 28, South of Milford. This large tavern was constructed before 1813 by members of the Culley family, settlers who came to the area as early as 1772 to find a suitable mill site. Neglected for some years, the tavern has now deteriorated almost irreversibly. It is said to have been haunted by a peddler who hanged himself in a closet under the stairs.

148. RESIDENCE, Route 28, Portlandville. The strong cubical outline, ornamented fascia of the roof line, double brackets, bay window, and the long, lower parlor windows —all these are features found on other Italianate residences in Otsego County. This one stands out as remarkably intact in a village which has suffered architecturally and environmentally from the widening of Main Street and excessive renovations of many buildings.

149. **Preston House, Route 28, South of Milford Center.** Built in 1827 by Colonel Alfred Mumford, this unusual version of a Greek Revival house has been considered a landmark by architectural historians. The false window with elliptical fan in the center of the façade is echoed in the semicircular fan in the broken pediment. Recent work has done much to preserve the exterior of the building.

Town of Oneonta

150. **BRIMMER FARM, Route 48, between Oneonta and Otego.** The first structure built by John and Martha Brimmer was of logs, set just west of the present frame house. This permanent home was put up in 1813. With a deep plan, steeply pitched gables, and lack of ornamentation, it is characteristic of the period of early settlement. Although removed now, the house at one time had a central chimney for heating and cooking. Remodeling took place during the 1840s. The recessed doorway with its square pilasters is typically Greek Revival.

151. EMMONS STONE HOUSE, Route 7, Emmons. Ira Emmons, a hops and lumber dealer and prominent early settler, started building this home in 1817. It was completed in 1821. A combination of stylistic influences, its plan is suggestive of the Georgian style, but the entranceway and details are typically Federal. Since its construction the house has been considered a local landmark — it has also undergone several remodelings. Before the house was built an agreement with the stonemason was drawn up promising him, among other things, a half-pint of whiskey a day while at work.

152. COLLISCROFT, Route 28, South of Oneonta. Built in 1904 by Edmund Pardee, a railroad executive, this imposing example of the Neo-Classical Revival is situated on a hill overlooking Oneonta. It was named to honor Collis P. Huntington, Pardee's relative, famous for the development of the Southern Pacific Railroad.

City of Oneonta and the Walnut Street Historic District

During the last decades of the nineteenth century the city of Oneonta was remarkably transformed from a rural village into a large and prosperous market center. From that time it has remained the most urbanized part of the county, drawing population and commercial activity from outlying areas.

The landmarks in the city are numerous, although recent development has obliterated or altered some of the most significant. Existing landmarks range from the oldest surviving pioneer home within city limits, the Swart-Wilcox House (plate 153), to a grand example of octagonal building, the Bull House on Division Street (plate 168). Unfortunately, important structures associated with the city's role as an educational center have been demolished or entirely altered: "Old Main," the oldest State Normal School structure in the state (plates 25 and 26), and the Willard E. Yager "Longhouse Museum," which was built to house the Yager Collection of Indian Artifacts now at Hartwick College.

There are several extant structures associated with the important role that Oneonta played as a center of railroad activity, including the skeleton of what was once the largest roundhouse in the world (plate 18). Oneonta was the section of the county most visibly affected by the railroad. Population increased tenfold in two decades; soon what had once been a small hamlet dwarfed all the adjacent communities, as reflected in the grandeur of the Oneonta Hotel (plates 156 and 157), erected in 1909.

The commercial section of Oneonta's Main Street was, at one time, one of the finest groupings of late nineteenth-century commercial buildings in the region. The rich detailing, the variety of brick patterning, the uniformity of height, and the delightful contrasts of texture and facade treatment — all set Oneonta's Main Street apart. Well-meaning developers and citizens did not fully realize the value of these structures until irreversible changes had been wrought. Ironically, preservation consciousness has only recently surfaced, too late to prevent much destruction. Perhaps the visual impact of Oneonta's redevelopment experience will prevent similar occurrences in other communities.

Along Main Street several important public buildings have survived, thus far, intact. The most significant of these are the Old Post Office Building (plate 160) and the Municipal Building (plates 158 and 159), both outstanding architectural achievements of their respective periods.

It is in the residential sections of the city that representative dwellings from the late nineteenth and early twentieth centuries can be found. In the late 1800s both wealthy and middle-class Oneontans could afford to build expansive homes. Although collectively called Victorian, these homes represent a variety of styles. Local architects began with the traditions of Europe (Gothic, Second Empire) and developed a myriad of eclectic combinations. Mass production allowed for the proliferation of decorative wooden and brick homes, each one distinct from the others.

The rich and varied collection of historic buildings lining Walnut Street in Oneonta may be regarded as an environmental resource, a neighborhood with unique historic and visual character. While some of the structures are distinctive individually, it is the blend of styles, their near-original condition, and their gracious surroundings which make the neighborhood a historic district. District designation at the national level is intended to contribute to public awareness and concern that will prevent needless destruction or change, and to stimulate interest in preserving this and other historic areas of the city.

153. Swart-Wilcox House, Wilcox Avenue, Oneonta. The oldest standing structure (1807) in the city of Oneonta, the Swart-Wilcox House has undergone changes and additions. However, the saltbox outline is clearly visible, and the side door retains its original hood moldings. Situated on a virtually unspoiled site, it may become the focus of a park and museum complex.

154. Yager House, 307 Chestnut Street, Oneonta. The George H. Yager farmhouse was built between 1830 and 1840. While it is surprising to find an example of a Greek Revival farmhouse within the confines of a growing city, it is nevertheless a fact that at one time Oneonta was a small village (Milfordville) with a high concentration of Greek Revival buildings. A limited number of these have survived, some on River Street; the interested observer must look carefully to find these traces of the city's past.

155. ARMORY, 4 Academy Street, Oneonta. The Armory was first constructed in 1885, later remodeled in 1893. The building reflects the turn-of-the-century interest in the Richardsonian or Romanesque style, which projected a massive, fortresslike image. In this case the style was most appropriate. The rough stonework, the round-headed windows, and the castlelike tower all contribute to the strength of the building.

156. Main Street, Oneonta. Carefully designed, with consideration for detail and utilizing various technological advances, the commercial and public buildings which exist today in Otsego County range from the simplest craft shop to the ornate county courthouse. The late nineteenth- and twentieth-century examples are the ones most vulnerable to development at present. The commercial section of Oneonta has been almost irreversibly affected by demolition and alteration. Still visible landmarks are the Oneonta Hotel, left, which has been altered at ground level but which retains its grand details and massive proportions (plate 157), and the Woolworth Building, with its intricate and varied cornice decoration.

157. ONEONTA HOTEL, Detail, 195 Main Street, Oneonta. The most ambitious structure erected in Oneonta's commercial section was the Oneonta Hotel, completed in 1909. It was built at a time when many elements of different periods in Western European architecture were being combined in diverse ways—leading to the heavily decorated Beaux-Arts style. The building originally had three arched entrances at street level, but one has been destroyed in order to make an entrance to Woolworth's. A row of lions' heads gazes down from just below the roof line.

158. **Municipal Building, 242 Main Street, Oneonta.** The formality and classical elements of its design make this building particularly appropriate as the seat of city government. Built in 1906, it is an outstanding mix of turn-of-the-century Neo-Classical Revival and Beaux-Arts styles. A formal design and an elaborate granite trim make it a grand component of the central business district. The tower was recently added as a Bicentennial project and is a replica of one which stood on an adjacent landmark, the Westcott Building, destroyed in 1969.

159. MUNICIPAL BUILDING, Detail. The detail of the entranceway shows the quality of craftsmanship expended on the center of city government. Photo courtesy of *The Daily Star*, Oneonta, N.Y.

160. OLD POST OFFICE, Main Street and Ford Avenue, Oneonta. This massive masonry building was constructed in 1913 of Indiana limestone and Concord granite trim. It constitutes an important element in the streetscape in Oneonta, particularly since the unfortunate removal of many of the commercial center's best architectural features. With an impressive pillared design, it contributes an air of dignity and grandeur characteristic of Neo-Classical Revival public buildings of the early twentieth century. The City of Oneonta, present owner of the building, is working with planners to ascertain the best re-use for the building. The building has been approved at the state level for listing on the National Register of Historic Places.

161. 21, 23, 25 ELM STREET, Walnut Street Historic District, Oneonta.
These three houses on the south side of Elm Street are part of the Walnut Street Historic District. While none of them is individually outstanding, the ensemble that they create is a significant part of the residential environment in the city. Other streets nearby have equally interesting structures — all important to preserve insofar as the loss of one affects the quality of the setting for all of the others. Here on Elm Street the Rowe House (1898), right, with its well-proportioned Neo-Classical Revival details, contrasts with the adjacent Smith House (1870), center, a Second Empire structure, and its similar neighbor, the Moody House (1870), left.

162. WILBER MANSION, 11 Ford Avenue, Walnut Street Historic District, Oneonta. An important local businessman, George I. Wilber, began construction of this house in 1875. It originally had a flat roof but was remodeled in the 1890s in the then-fashionable Queen Anne mode. The round tower with its flaring cornice placed at the corner of the building, the steep pitch of the roof and the extra gable, and the shaping of the porch to wrap around all sides of the house were characteristics common to Queen Anne structures. No less important is the intricate patterning of the facade, creating a textured surface. Fortunately, the house has been the focus of community preservation efforts, resulting in its current re-use for city offices.

163. BARNES-BUTTS HOUSE, 35 Ford Avenue, Walnut Street Historic District, Oneonta. This structure, also within the boundaries of the historic district, was owned by a succession of important local business families. Exhibiting a combination of Pictorial Eclectic and Queen Anne details, the house is distinctive for its decorative chimneys, the plaques set in the facade, the variations in surface texture, and the stained glass windows.

165. 17, 19, 21 WALNUT STREET, Walnut Street Historic District, Oneonta.
These three buildings demonstrate how structures of varying styles can complement one another. The Harrieff House, right, built c. 1870 and at one time used as a storehouse for hops, contrasts with the imposing Hemstreet-Pendleton House, center, which was constructed in 1904 with full-blown Neo-Classical Revival details. Across Dietz Street is the Moore House, left, an important example of the Queen Anne style, built in 1895. The latter is notable for the varied use of surface materials (rough-cut stone, chipped brick, and wood strips) and for its extra dormers and gables.

164. GOULD-KELLOGG HOUSE, 29 Ford Avenue, Walnut Street Historic District, Oneonta. Built in 1882 for Frank Gould, a local businessman, for some years this was the residence of Supreme Court Justice A. L. Kellogg. It is a most elaborate example of Pictorial Eclecticism, with rich decorations and complex form. The intricate porches, the high-pitched roofs, the patterned brickwork, and the ironwork cresting contribute to the picturesque quality of the building.

166. **Stable, Oak Street, Oneonta.** As Oneonta prospered in the latter part of the nineteenth century, there was much traffic through the town. Of the several large livery stables maintained, this is the largest one to have survived. The cupola retains decorative Victorian details.

167. **Fairchild Mansion, 318 Main Street, Oneonta.** Built in 1867, this is one of two Oneonta buildings on the National Register of Historic Places. First built as a flat-roofed dwelling, it was remodeled in the Queen Anne style in 1891 by George W. Fairchild, a United States congressman and one of the original promotors of International Business Machines. Now the Masonic Temple, the building retains, in its interior, many elegant features. No expense was spared in outfitting the building, as shown in the use of Belgian tiles on the roof. Despite the disruptive effects of a nearby motel and gasoline stations, the mansion maintains an aura of grandeur.

169. THE DEPOT, 4½ Railroad Avenue, Oneonta. Railroad stations are fast becoming obsolete: this typical railroad station has been successfully adapted for use as a restaurant. The exterior is essentially intact, and the interior has been designed to incorporate many original features.

168. BULL HOUSE, 16 Division Street, Oneonta. This elaborate example of an octagonal structure is surmounted by a mansard roof and intricate cupola. The writer Orson Squire Fowler, a leading practitioner of phrenology, popularized the form in his 1848 book *A Home for All*. Otsego County boasts several surviving octagonal buildings, the last of which in Oneonta was built in 1870.

Town and Village of Otego

170. **BIRDSALL-HOYT FARM, Route I-88, near Junction with Route 48, Town of Otego.** The economy of Otsego County has always been focused on agricultural products, primarily dairy products, but also on wheat, corn, pork, wool, and hops. Outbuildings such as dairy barns, corn cribs, sheep pens, and smokehouses reflect these concerns. The Birdsall-Hoyt farmstead is a typical working complex which includes a small farmhouse, left, built in the early nineteenth century, a succession of barns ranging from the 1820s to the large Victorian barn built in 1870, and a modern silo.

171. **PALMER-HUNT HOUSE, 36 Main Street, Otego.** Near the center of Otego is this well-proportioned Greek Revival structure, used originally as a residence and briefly as an annex for the local school. Constructed in 1844, it has features common to many Greek Revival buildings: broad entablature with dentils, square columns supporting a one-story porch, and recessed door framed by sidelights. The cupola is a feature seen on other large, late Greek Revival structures with square plans. The house now serves as the Roland B. Hill Archaeological Museum, developed by the Upper Susquehanna Chapter of the New York Archaeological Association.

173. **IMMANUEL PROTESTANT EPISCOPAL CHURCH, Church Street, Otego.** The long windows and their Gothic outlines are the only remaining evidences of stylistic design on this simple stone church built in 1836. Now used for storage, the structure is still sound and could be creatively rehabilitated.

172. **PRESBYTERIAN CHURCH, River Street, Otego.** The Presbyterian Church is an example of the high level of sophistication which certain local builders achieved in the Upper Susquehanna region in the early nineteenth century. This meetinghouse has the fine proportions and refined details that distinguish craftsmen from builders. Here eighteenth-century designs have been followed in part — perhaps based on the well-known pattern books by Asher Benjamin — and combined with the Greek Revival custom of placing the tower above the main roof. The entire building is enriched by delicate detailing characteristic of the Federal period and surmounted by a skillfully designed four-stage tower-belfry. The result is a unique transitional structure. Church records show that the congregation was established in 1805 and the building erected in 1833. The interior includes an original gallery on two sides and an arched ceiling. There is some evidence, as yet not conclusive, that the church was designed by the Rockwell brothers, builders known to have constructed the Gilbertsville Grange Hall, formerly a Presbyterian Church (plate 115), which is similar in plan and detailing.

174. BUNDY TAVERN, Junction of Secour Road and Route 7, Otego.
The tavern, kept by two sons of Captain Peter Bundy, a friend of Judge William Cooper who came into the valley in 1786 from Massachusetts, is an excellent example of the numerous taverns which once served travelers along early plank roads and turnpikes. Now a residence, the tavern is unmistakably Federal in style. It has slim proportions, reeded corner pilasters, and broad doorway with semielliptical fanlight over the door and sidelights. The tavern was a major stop on the stage which ran between Emmons and Unadilla, and it is said that wealthy southern planters with their families and slaves stopped here regularly on their way to Saratoga Springs. During Abraham Lincoln's second presidential campaign, William Seward, then secretary of state, spoke on Lincoln's behalf from the tavern steps.

Town of Unadilla

175. MILFER FARM OR FERRY MANSION, Junction of Butternut Road and Route 3A, Unadilla Center. This early nineteenth-century stone farmhouse was remodeled in 1890 by Albert Kahn, an industrial architect from Detroit, as a summer residence for Dexter M. Ferry, owner of the famous seed company in Detroit. Kahn also designed the "Honeymoon Cottage" on the property, one of the earliest prefabricated houses built.

176. SILVERNAIL BARN, Route 1, between Route 7 and East Guilford.
Agricultural structures varied less in form and function than other types of buildings. Those built in the early nineteenth century in Otsego County had little ornamentation. This 1890 barn is typical of the barns built toward the end of the century, when at least the outline of openings and certain detailed structural elements were elaborated. Typical late nineteenth-century cupolas were added here as well.

177. WELLHOUSE, DeCalvin-Buker Tavern, Route 7, between Unadilla and Sidney.
Many taverns were located along the route of the original Catskill Turnpike. The DeCalvin-Buker Tavern, said to have been built in 1795, served as an inn until 1860. The main structure is well known for its finely crafted interior woodwork and its seven fireplaces. As a structure which was once essential for every homestead, this outbuilding still retains its original wooden wheel.

178. TIANDERAH, off Butternut Road, Northeast of Unadilla. This landmark was built in 1875–78 for H. Y. Canfield, a local inventor. Approximately twenty years later it was sold and used as a resort, a "sporting house," and a gambling casino. It was part of a carefully designed park with riding and walking trails, gardens, plantings, and an artificial lake. The house commands a sweeping view of the Susquehanna River, and it combines elements of both the Queen Anne and Shingle styles—an important example of vernacular construction on a grand scale. The building has always been known as Tianderah—one translation of the word meaning "meeting place."

Village of Unadilla

The village of Unadilla is notable for a wide range of buildings of special architectural and historic interest. While an identified historic district has not yet been documented, a major portion of the village would certainly qualify as such. A historic district would essentially extend along Main Street, from the eastern edge of the village to the railroad tracks at the western edge, and include many of the adjacent side streets. Within this area there are elegant homes built by early settlers, distinctive late nineteenth-century commercial blocks, and fine examples of vernacular forms of nineteenth-century styles.

Most of the structures in the village are frame buildings, with several important stone buildings, and a sampling of brick commercial structures. There are outstanding architectural achievements and many intact country structures. Generally compatible in scale and form and well-maintained, these buildings combine with the community's riverside setting to create one of the most pleasing village environments in Otsego County.

The location of Unadilla at the confluence of the Susquehanna and Unadilla rivers has been a critical element in its growth. Near the site of an eighteenth-century Indian settlement, the present village really developed as a result of turnpike traffic. "Wattle's Ferry" was maintained at the mouth of the Ouleout Creek in the 1790s, and it wasn't long before this became the western-most terminus of the main road westward from the Hudson. The Catskill Turnpike provided direct access to regions farther south and west. The growth of the village, therefore, reflected westward movement through New York State.

Unadilla grew rapidly in the first two decades of the nineteenth century, from a tiny settlement in 1804 to a village of substantial homes in 1815, well known to visitors from beyond the area. Dr. Timothy Dwight, president of Yale College, passed through Unadilla twice between 1804 and 1815 and observed the rapid development of the community: "Unadilla is becoming a very pretty village ... and the number of houses, particularly of good ones, has much increased."

Throughout most of the nineteenth century Unadilla served as a marketing center for the surrounding area. After the introduction of the railroad, growth increased considerably. Products already manufactured locally began to be produced on a large scale; a local creamery, for instance, prospered. Much of the commercial area with its outstanding brick blocks dates from this era.

179. WHITE HOUSE, 14 Main Street (Old Route 7), Unadilla. This unusual example of early construction in the county was built by the Cone brothers from Hebron, Connecticut, in 1815. The L-shaped plan, the Palladian windows, and detailed entablature signify its connection with more sophisticated structures in New England.

180. North-Lyon House, 102 Main Street, Unadilla. Colonel S. S. North built this handsome home in 1865. The brackets and woodwork are similar to several other elegant Italianate buildings in Unadilla. The cast-iron dogs on the front steps are considered local landmarks.

181. 1879 BLOCK, Main Street, Unadilla. Not long ago many communities in Otsego County had commercial structures similar to this one lining their main streets. The varied roofline, heavily decorated cornice, and brick patterning, as well as the outlines of the original store fronts make this a special feature of Unadilla.

182. 66, 64, 62 MAIN STREET, Unadilla. Along the length of Unadilla's Main Street are substantial residences from all periods in the community's history. This grouping near the center of the village conveys the sense of solidity and prosperity that is evident elsewhere. The two stone structures, left and right, were built within five years of one

another; the son of one of the owners built the later house between them, center. Thus the growth of a family as well as a community is reflected in the changes in architectural style: Greek Revival buildings were superseded by Shingle style houses towards the end of the century. The Noble-Sands House, right, the largest and most significant of the grouping, was built around 1865 by George H. Noble, a successful merchant. The house has strong and well-proportioned features, from the porch supported by simple Doric columns, to the plainly paneled entablature, to the cupola with its dentils and pilasters. This is important as an example of late Greek Revival construction and as a visual element of the streetscape in Unadilla.

183. "Lily Vale" or Fancher House, 21 Watson Street, Unadilla. One of the small number of octagonal buildings left in Otsego County, this residence was constructed before 1868 by Selek H. Fancher, a local shoemaker.

184. **YORK CORPORATION (CANFIELD CREAMERY), Mill Street and Watson Street, Unadilla.** H. Y. Canfield, a local inventor, had a well-known creamery in this building, built in 1860. Here he devised and operated an early process for producing condensed milk. The creamery, which ran well into the twentieth century, is typical of the industrial structures built in the postrailroad era, patterned after the large commercial structures of the same period. These were usually two- or three-story brick structures with patterning at the roof line, arched window openings, and long rhythmic façades. Like earlier industrial buildings they emphasized function rather than appearance.

185. UNADILLA SILO, Clifton Street and Sperry Street, Unadilla. This structure is part of the complex run by the VanCott family who have had, in succession, on this site a planing mill and feed store; a flour, feed, lumber, and shingle business; and currently a plant for the manufacture of silos. The large frame building dates from the last quarter of the nineteenth century.

186. Freight House, Railroad Street and Depot Street, Unadilla.
Railroad structures are a special category of buildings which are becoming obsolete. The few existing railroad stations, such as this 1866 depot in Unadilla with its typical overhanging roof, have either been abandoned or remodeled extensively.

188. Hotel Bishop, 28 Main Street, Unadilla. Unadilla was an important stopping off point for westward travelers since its early days. This hotel has housed travelers from midcentury on up to the present day. It bears the typical features of commercial and public establishments built in the postrailroad era, such as the patterned brickwork and the slightly arched windows.

187. St. Matthew's Episcopal Church, 33 Main Street, Unadilla.
During and after the mid-nineteenth century the addition of Gothic features to early classical churches was a common practice, allowing local carpenters to display their skills at executing elaborate motifs in wood. St. Matthew's Church, originally constructed in 1814, is a simple classical form totally draped in Gothic trim. St. Matthew's was started in 1810, but owing to lack of local funds it stood partially completed until 1814 when Trinity Parish of New York City gave sufficient money for its completion.

190. **BEACH-DOKUCHITZ HOUSE, 1 Main Street, Unadilla.** Set at the northern end of the village just on the banks of the Susquehanna River is one of the oldest structures in the village. It has been enlarged several times, but portions of the main block date from before 1802. The small park and landscaped setting enhance the house, as does the nearby Susquehanna River.

189. **MEEKER HOUSE, 25 Main Street, Unadilla.** This striking home is located near the center of the village of Unadilla. Built for Roswell Wright, an early merchant, the house has been owned by prominent local political and business families. Despite the intrusions of nearby traffic and commercial activity, the house has retained its original exterior features, including the arched fanlight and rich glass detailing of the front entranceway and the unusual and beautifully scrolled brackets in support of the pediment. The house bears a strong resemblance to a residence on Main Street in Franklin, a community located on the west bank of the Unadilla River in neighboring Delaware County. It is possible that the same builder crafted both houses.

191. HAYES HOUSE, 14 Main Street, Unadilla. In 1805 the Reverend Timothy Dwight remarked that the home of Isaac Hayes was "the finest house west of Catskill on the Catskill Turnpike." The house has had some unfortunate renovations — the most outstanding being the addition of artificial stone siding — but the early plan and some original Federal and Georgian features such as this portico and doorway can still be seen. Hayes maintained a successful business shipping lumber and grains to southern markets down the Susquehanna River, and the family remained socially and politically prominent for several generations.

7

SCHENEVUS CREEK VALLEY

THE SCHENEVUS CREEK VALLEY, encompassing the townships of Maryland, Decatur, and Worcester at the southeastern edge of the county, was settled before the Revolutionary War. Some of the first mills in the county were erected in this region, and early transportation routes which roughly paralleled the Schenevus Creek were important for the movement of produce and goods southward to the Susquehanna River.

Before 1850 there was little development in this farming valley. Small communities along the creek were surrounded by outlying farmsteads, many of which still remain today. These are usually very simple in style, with Georgian or Federal proportions and modest detailing (plate 196). Greek Revival structures, although common, are not as predominant in this region as in other parts of the county, probably because the region never developed the kinds of active manufacturing centers in the 1830s and 1840s which grew up in other parts of the county. The Greek Revival structures which do exist, however, include both modest (plate 204) and ambitious examples (plate 206).

The construction of the railroad through the Schenevus Creek Valley in 1865 caused an economic boom. The village of Worcester, formerly a modest collection of homes and an inn, grew rapidly during the 1870s and 1880s, as did the village of Schenevus. The commercial and residential buildings dating from this time clearly record the commercial impact of the railroad and the prevailing eclectic styles. Houses had wonderfully irregular shapes (plate 212), store fronts had fanciful sawed or brick patterned decorations (plate 198), and even outbuildings such as the Robinson House stable reveal the talents of local builders (plate 215). It is important to remember that in this region, as in every other section of the county, few structures were stylistically pure. Especially after the midcentury, builders were inclined to combine elements from various popular styles. Many hybrid or transitional buildings can be found; these are often the most exciting to observe (plate 194).

With the growth of Schenevus and Worcester, other communities in the region became overshadowed. Their social functions have continued, but their economic functions have abated if not disappeared altogether. This is reflected in the number of unused or abandoned structures in the small, remote hamlets.

Some small communities, however, have retained their own identities, as much because of their architectural character as because of their social functions. South Worcester, with its particular blend of classical building forms, is a case in point. Even the smallest hamlets—Maryland, East Worcester, and Decatur—contain a mix of public and private structures from the early and mid-nineteenth century which continue to serve community needs.

Through the twentieth century the valley has retained its essentially agricultural character, as symbolized by the large dairy barns which dot the landscape (plate 195). With the construction of I-88, some farmlands will be taken from the region, but the diverse landmarks which contribute to the aesthetic character of the Schenevus Valley are increasingly being recognized and protected.

Town of Maryland

192, 193. DISTRICT SCHOOL NO. 12, off Route 7, Town of Maryland.
The two details shown here represent typical features of Italianate structures built throughout the county in the 1850s and 1860s. The abandoned schoolhouse has recently been demolished as a result of the construction of I-88.

194. RESIDENCE, Route 7, between Colliersville and Maryland.
During the mid-nineteenth century there was such a proliferation of styles that much overlap occurred, even on a single structure. This vernacular residence is an interesting blend of styles which needs careful reading. The basic T-shape plan, the flushboard siding, and the classical molding at the roof line are all Greek Revival features. The recessed doorway with arched outline and sidelights dates back to the even earlier Federal period, and the quoins, or blocks used at the corners to simulate stones, are Georgian characteristics. The brackets are Italianate, as are the details on the entrance canopy and the window cornices. The Neo-Tuscan columns supporting the porch are unusual and could have been used during the Italianate period.

195. BARN, Route 7, South of Maryland. The typical Otsego County barn did not emphasize appearance as much as function. Construction techniques — traditional "barn framing" or the mortise and tenon frame — and plan — usually three bays with gabled roof—did not vary greatly through most of the century. The large Victorian barns of the last quarter of the nineteenth century often had decorative cupolas and ornamentation at the openings similar to that found on domestic buildings. This barn, constructed c. 1870, reflects the typical Victorian building style in scale and detail as well as the growing reliance on dairy farming.

196. GODDARD HOUSE, Elk Creek Road, North of Schenevus. Edward Goddard came to the Schenevus area about 1793. He was the first tanner and currier and the first boot and shoemaker. His tannery was located nearby on Elk Creek. His early homestead, a vernacular version of the Federal style, retains original features including some of the early panes of glass which are twelve over twelve and an arched entranceway with detached sidelights.

197. KEYES-TIPPLE HOUSE, 27 Main Street, Schenevus. An unusually ambitious house, this was built for the wife of Washington Keyes in the early 1890s. No expense was spared in outfitting the structure both inside and out with the latest fashions, from a festooned Palladian window to French wallpaper. The house and contents are still intact. The elaborate classical details illustrate the popular interest in reviving the aesthetic aspects of America's colonial past.

198. 54, 56 MAIN STREET, Commercial Buildings, Schenevus.
These commercial buildings date from the 1880s and represent yet another instance of the decorative quality of late nineteenth-century main streets. There is an extraordinary interplay of window shapes, cornice treatments, and applied motifs, versions of which can be discovered on other contemporary main streets behind obtrusive signs and wires.

199. Main Street Buildings, 50 and 52 Main Street, Schenevus.
These buildings display the same continuity of design and harmonious relationship which marks the street in Morris (plate 107) and other villages. Note the alternating large and small scrolled brackets decorating the projecting cornice of the hardware store.

201. GRISWOLD HOUSE, Route 7, between Schenevus and Worcester.
Elijah Griswold settled in the town of Maryland in 1807 and built this substantial permanent home c. 1815. It is said that the stone was brought from an East Worcester quarry by ox cart. The plan is basically Federal—doorway with fanlight, symmetrical facade, pitched roof, and end chimneys. The wing, half of which was an open woodshed with an elliptical opening since enclosed, was built in the mid-ninteenth century. Photograph courtesy of Robert Hage.

200. GRABLEWYN, 101 Main Street, Schenevus. This dignified village residence was first constructed during the mid-nineteenth century but remodeled in 1909. Note the unusual balustrade on the roof line, the cupola, and the portico.

Town of Worcester

202. DOCTOR'S OFFICE, Route 40, South Worcester. For some rural villages local doctors were a fixture of community life (plate 75). During the nineteenth century two different doctors practiced medicine in this small Greek Revival building, with its fluted entrance columns and corner pilasters. The simplicity of the lines and the clear expression of purpose make this a striking element in the local landscape. The building was moved to its present site and converted quite successfully for use as a private library.

203. METHODIST CHURCH, Route 40, South Worcester. This is a vernacular, simplified version of the New England meetinghouse plan exhibiting elements of both the Federal and Greek Revival periods. The hexagonal cupola is suggestive of Italianate forms.

204. GENERAL STORE, Route 40, South Worcester. Somewhat similar to the Methodist Church (plate 203), with the same plain, squared-off Greek features, this store building is similar to numerous other commercial and public buildings constructed with modified temple shapes during the Greek Revival era.

205. Cabinet Shop, Route 40, South Worcester. This modest structure, built for an essential local craft, exemplifies the simplicity of plan and design which characterized the earliest preindustrial structures.

206. CARYL'S STORE, Main Street (Route 7), East Worcester. When this large brick building was constructed in 1841 by Leonard Caryl, it was the most elegant and expensive structure in the vicinity. It was dubbed "Caryl's Folly" due to its huge size, and for many years it served as a residence and general store. Note the fine Greek Revival features, including the three pairs of columns "in antis" (within).

207. STONE MILL, Mill Street, Worcester. On the banks of the Schenevus Creek just southeast of the village of Worcester is one of the last surviving examples of an early gristmill in the county. With strong, simple lines and of sturdy fieldstone construction, this structure typifies the many industrial buildings constructed as the county was undergoing vast expansion in the 1820s and 1830s. The mill was built c. 1830 on a hump of land known locally as "Hog's Back." Because the water behind the dam fell too low during dry weather a steam plant was eventually installed in the mill. This mill supplied the first electric power for the village in 1889, an event likened to "Fairyland" in newspaper accounts. The structure is now unused and somewhat deteriorated. However, the setting and the basically strong frame of the building make it an ideal candidate for adaptive re-use.

The Worcester Historic District

The village of Worcester is located at the eastern edge of Otsego County at the junction of the Schenevus and Decatur creeks. The commercial center of the village, the historic district, extends along both sides of Main Street containing frame and brick buildings from the late nineteenth and early twentieth centuries which constitute an unusually rich and intact grouping. The value of this historic district is the representative picture that it presents of a late nineteenth-century village main street.

The historic district is vital in the ongoing life of the community—the buildings are utilized fully for businesses, entertainment, and residences. The buildings are in scale with the world of the pedestrian, being but two stories in height. The twenty-odd buildings complement one another, and their close proximity leads to pleasing contrasts in mass, texture, and outline. The highly decorative facades are products of the new tools and wood-working techniques available to local builders. With the exception of some street-level show windows, alterations have been minimal.

208. WIGHTMAN BUILDING, 83 Main Street, Worcester Historic District, Worcester.
The Wightman Building is notable for its richly decorated wooden facade which displays the skill of the local carpenter. The original motifs have been especially well preserved.

209. Main Street, Worcester Historic District, Worcester. The Worcester Historic District extends along both sides of Main Street to include the entire commercial section. The public and commercial buildings exemplify the construction trends of the late nineteenth century, a time of rapid growth resulting from the railroad.

210. SMITH AND SWARTOUT BUILDING, Main Street, Worcester Historic District, Worcester. In the center of Main Street is this striking example of brick commercial architecture built in 1884. From the original street-level fronts (with appropriately modest signs) to the intact roof line with its intricate iron cresting and finials, this building has retained features which were once common to many main street stores.

211. FIREHOUSE, Worcester Historic District, Worcester. Simultaneous with the Shingle style toward the end of the nineteenth century was a tendency to decorate façades with wooden strips in varying patterns. This Stick style treatment can be seen on the old firehouse building in Worcester.

212. Rowley-Sloan Residence, 127 Main Street, Worcester Historic District, Worcester. At the northern end of the historic district is one of the most decorative of the five residences in the district. Here stylistic details are blended to create a unique design: a mansard roof is combined with steeply pitched roofs, and the gables are trimmed with bargeboards and the roof ridges with metal cresting. The heavy pedimented window molding and bracketed bay window are an added interest.

213. CARRIAGE HOUSE, Main Street, Worcester Historic District, Worcester.
The carriage house belonging to the Gothic residence known as the Wilson Place on Main Street is unique in its conception and detailing. The builder is said to have been a McLaughlin, perhaps responsible as well for some of the other intricately worked mid-century structures within Worcester's historic district.

214. ROBINSON MANSION, Main Street, Worcester Historic District, Worcester.
Along upper Main Street are substantial homes built in the various styles of the nineteenth century. These contrast with and complement the commercial buildings at the lower end of Main Street. This Greek Revival dwelling, built in 1832 by James Robinson, was part of a great estate with English gardens, peacocks, and rare trees.

The temple front of the house projects from a massive rectangular block; the paneled pilasters repeat the rhythm of the four Doric columns. Ornamentation is kept to a minimum. As a statement of solidity and success, the house demonstrates the usefulness of Greek forms that vernacular binders varied in proportion and detail to reflect the life'style of the owner.

215. BARN, Main Street, Worcester Historic District, Worcester. The barn which was part of the Robinson mansion complex has unusually decorative features for an outbuilding. Constructed in the 1870s, this is a noteworthy Stick style example of local talent. The small structure in the foreground was moved from a location near the mansion where it had housed the waterworks for the property.

8

CHERRY VALLEY REGION

THE CHERRY VALLEY REGION extends from the plateau above the Mohawk River at the northeastern edge of the county southward to encompass the townships of Middlefield, Roseboom, Westford, and Cherry Valley. Divided by the Cherry Valley Creek, the region is well known for its special physical qualities. The picturesque valley surrounded by broad forested hills provides the setting for a handful of isolated villages, rural residences, and agricultural units. The village of Cherry Valley is the largest community in the region; it has traditionally served as the focus of social and commercial activity for the predominantly agricultural adjacent areas.

  The Cherry Valley region was settled early as it was on the main route southward from the major east-west turnpikes. Cherry Valley itself was a hub of passenger traffic and for the movement of goods and produce westward. The region was never directly affected by the commercial activity which took place in the Schenevus Creek Valley and the Upper Susquehanna River Basin after the railroad was introduced into those areas.

  The historic structures which can be found today in the Cherry Valley region record the pattern of early development and subsequent stabilization. Due to its location near the Mohawk Valley and more settled sections of the state, there are more very early (late eighteenth-century) structures in the northeast part of the region than in most other parts of the county (plate 227). There are also more substantial dwellings which date from the very first part of the nineteenth century (plate 7), evidences of the tastes of those who settled in the region. The eastern parts of the Cherry Valley region have always been sparsely populated, with traffic oriented in a north-south rather than an east-west direction, and with rugged hills making communication difficult. Hamlets such as Westford and South Valley are still relatively isolated and contain structures which date primarily from before 1850. Along the Cherry Valley Creek development is slightly more evident, although such communities as Roseboom and Middlefield also exhibit structures from the early part of the century.

Overall the character of the region is largely determined by the blend of natural and structural resources, both of which have been relatively well preserved and which constitute a historic landscape worthy of careful study and future conservation.

Towns of Roseboom and Westford

217. Residence, Stannard Road, near Junction with Route 165, Town of Roseboom. This unusual structure combines both stone and frame construction. The stone section, probably dating from the 1850s, has simplified Italianate characteristics, and while there are Italianate structures in the county which are basically square in plan, the use of stone is rare. The frame wing may date from a later period.

216. Greek Revival Residence, Gage Road, near Junction with Route 165, Town of Roseboom. A common Greek Revival house plan was the two-story central block with balanced wings. On this vernacular residence the temple front section has a recessed lower portion with columns "in antis" below the outlined pediment.

219. **THE DRAPER ACADEMY, County Route 34, Westford.** Formerly known as the Literary Institute, this large Greek Revival school building was renamed after Andrew S. Draper, a native of Westford, who became the first commissioner of education in New York State and a president of the University of Illinois.

218. **GRIGGS STORE, Junction of County Route 34 and Middlefield Road, Westford.** There are many Greek Revival stores located in Otsego County, a reminder that the style was considered appropriate for all kinds of buildings. The store in Westford is one of the most representative, as well as intact, examples of a local general store. The interior is distinguished by its original shelving lining three walls; the tiers of shelves are supported on rows of tiny Greek columns. The building has been in continuous use as a store since about 1830. Note the similarities and differences between this building and its formal counterpart, the Otsego County Bank building in Cooperstown (plate 10).

221. Gothic Residence, Route 35, Westville. Gothic cottages became popular in the late 1840s and 1850s. Here the steep gables reveal the style's vertical emphasis, and the pierced bargeboards contribute to the picturesque effect.

220. Methodist Church, Route 34, Westford. The problem of dwindling congregations has resulted in the abandonment of many rural churches. This well-designed Greek Revival church is currently being used to store farm machinery.

Town of Middlefield

222. WOODSIDE HALL, Gate Tower, above Route 31, Cooperstown. The Gothic treatment of this gate tower reveals the popularity of the style for a variety of uses.

223. WOODSIDE HALL, Cooperstown. This elegant mansion, built in 1829 and associated with several well-known politicians of the nineteenth century, now serves as a nursing home. Modern additions do not detract from the special blend of Federal and Greek Revival features. President Martin Van Buren was a guest here in 1839.

224. OLD MIDDLEFIELD SCHOOLHOUSE, off Route 35, Middlefield. The District No. 1 schoolhouse in Middlefield has been successfully adapted for use as a community museum run by the Middlefield Historical Association. The schoolhouse was built in 1875 and has the bracketed cornices, steep gables, and bell tower common to many frame schools built in the post–Civil War period.

225. PINNEY'S TAVERN, Junction of Middlefield Road and Route 35, Middlefield.
The Federal structure which stands at the crossroads in Middlefield Center was maintained as a public house by Joshua L. Pinney as early as 1803. The tavern was the site of the first post office in the community and served for a brief period as headquarters for the local Masons. During the 1820s the pillars and two-story Greek Revival portico were added, and the parlor walls were decorated with a set of colorful pictorial murals, rare examples of American wall painting. The murals are attributed to William Price, who signed a set of similar murals found in the Carroll House in Springfield, just fifteen miles north of Middlefield. After 1842 the Pinney tavern became a residence and doctor's office; during the Civil War era sleighs and carriages were manufactured on the site.

226. KINGFISHER TOWER, Otsego Lake, Town of Middlefield. One of the unique architectural achievements in Otsego County is the Kingfisher Tower, erected in 1876 just off the eastern shore of Otsego Lake. It is far enough out into the lake to ensure that Cooperstonians gazing at it from the southern end of the lake, or anyone out on the lake itself, could see it clearly — a true landmark. The tower was constructed in the same spirit that octagonal buildings were: it was an attempt to experiment, to contribute something original to the building profession and to the landscape. The structure is pseudo-medieval in character, reminiscent of the castellated structures which were built along the banks of rivers and lakes in western Europe. The tower was not readily accepted by the community. Edward Clark, who had commissioned it, was driven to write the following in support of his work:

> Kingfisher tower consists of a miniature castle, after the style of the eleventh and twelfth centuries, standing upon the extremity of the Point and rising out of the water to a height of nearly sixty feet. It forms an objective point in the scene presented by the Lake and surrounding hills; it adds solemnity to the landscape, seeming to stand guard over the vicinity, while it gives a character of antiquity to the Lake, a charm by which we cannot help being impressed in such scenes. The effect of the structure is that of a picture from medieval times, and its value to the lake is very great. Mr. Clark has been led to erect it simply by desire to beautify the lake and add an attraction which must be seen by all who traverse the lake or drive along its shores. They, whose minds can rise above simple notions of utility to an appreciation of art joined to nature, will thank him for it.

Town of Cherry Valley

227. DUTCH BARN, Route 34A, East of Cherry Valley. This is the only known example of a Dutch barn left in Otsego County. Dutch barns are usually nearly square in plan and are characterized by H-beam construction on the inside. The H-frame is formed by a large, massive anchor beam which acts as a cross bearer and is unmatched in any other construction.

228. AUCHINBRECK, Campbell Road, North of Cherry Valley. This large, elegant home is on the site of the house built by the first permanent settler in Cherry Valley, James Campbell, as early as 1741. Colonel Samuel Campbell built a stockade in the same location which was destroyed in the Massacre of 1778. Two pyramids of ten-inch shells were placed in front of the house to mark the location of the stockade. The Campbell family, long influential in the village, has owned the site since the eighteenth century. George Washington visited here in 1783. Constructed in the late eighteenth century, the building has been enlarged several times.

Village of Cherry Valley

Cherry Valley is one of the best-known villages in Otsego County, indeed in Central New York. Nestled in the hills at the head of Cherry Valley Creek, the village was the site of the first white settlement south of the Mohawk River (1738). Events in Cherry Valley during the Revolutionary War were of national import. Throughout the period of permanent settlement after the war, Cherry Valley was a focal point for commercial and passenger traffic: by 1799 the Great Western Turnpike connecting Albany and Buffalo had been started. Extending as far as Cherry Valley, it was then called the Albany-Cherry Valley road.

Understandably, the village is rich in buildings of special architectural and historic interest. They range from the elegant homes of influential political and professional figures to public and commercial buildings which symbolize the community's role as an economic and transportation center. Other structural features of the landscape serve as reminders of the village's past: the two mortars which mark the entrance to Fort Alden, site of the famous Massacre of 1778 (Alden Street); and the Lithia Springs Pavilion, where a fountain brought from a nearby source the mineral waters which attracted visitors for many years (Alden Street).

While the majority of historic buildings in the village date from the first half of the nineteenth century, the period of greatest prosperity, there are also outstanding examples from later periods in the history of the community. The architectural characteristics of the village reflect its proximity to urban areas and the sophisticated life styles of the village's many prominent inhabitants. Many homes are constructed with more obvious concern for style and detail than is common in less accessible parts of the county. This was true at all periods, whether the structures were Federal in character, such as the Delos White House (plate 7), or from the Second Empire period, such as "The Alamo" (plate 236).

Although Cherry Valley's role as an economic center declined drastically in the late nineteenth century, the village has continued to attract loyal summer and year-round residents who appreciate the exceptional natural setting and the significant historic characteristics which make this a landmark village.

229. TOLL HOUSE, Cherry Valley. A historic view of the toll house before it was removed from its location spanning the Plank Road.

230. RESIDENCE (former Toll House), Route 166, South of Cherry Valley.
The Plank Road which ran for three and three-quarter miles between Cherry Valley and Roseboom was built in 1830 of hemlock planks and used for eighty-two years. This small toll house, which once stood near the present-day Route 166, controlled traffic along the Plank Road. It has now been moved back from the road and converted to a residence. Functional in form, the ornamentation at the eaves is characteristic of Gothic cottages built during the 1830s and 1840s.

231. OAKWOOD, Route 166, South of Cherry Valley. This unusual structure was built in the third decade of the nineteenth century by Franklin Campbell, a member of the Campbell family which was so influential in Cherry Valley's early history. The structure, now sadly deteriorated, is said to have been patterned after the ancestral home of the builder in Scotland. While the roof, cupola, and brackets suggest the Italianate style, the towers projecting from the two front corners and the huge, three-story size are more reminiscent of a European country estate.

232. STREETSCAPE, 81–87 Alden Street, Cherry Valley. The group of buildings which stands opposite Monument Square reflects the nature of the village as a manufacturing and social center for the region. The large Masonic Hall, right, was built in 1875 as the Union Hall and served for many years as a center where lectures, traveling minstrel shows, theatrical pieces, and even the first moving pictures were presented. The building has retained its original brackets, rows of arched windows, and at least the proportions of the original store fronts. The small building, center, was the first telegraph office in the area, set up by S. F. B. Morse with his associate Amos Swan.

233. BARRACKS OR BATE'S HOP HOUSE, Lancaster Street, Cherry Valley.
This unusual structure, built of rough stone in 1861, was used as a barracks for recruits in the early days of the Civil War. At one time almost 600 recruits from the area (one-tenth of the population enlisted) were quartered here. The building was later used as a hops barn.

Swan, who manufactured Cherry Valley melodeons in a building near this one, now demolished, had helped Morse construct the first telegraph machines. He later ran a school for telegraph operators in the Alden Street office and was instrumental in setting up one of the first telegraph lines in the country in 1844 which connected Albany and Syracuse.

234. CENTRAL NATIONAL BANK, Lancaster Street and Main Street, Cherry Valley.
In 1818 the National Central Bank of Cherry Valley was established, the oldest bank west of the Hudson and the first bank in the entire Cherry Valley and Upper Susquehanna region. It remained the only bank in the region until 1830, when the Otsego County Bank began operation in Cooperstown (plate 10). The bank started in a house owned by Levi Beardsley and shortly thereafter moved to its present building (now

235. COMMERCIAL BUILDINGS, 13–19 Main Street, Cherry Valley.
During the early and mid-nineteenth century Cherry Valley was a flourishing commercial and transportation center. This dignified row of intact commercial buildings testifies to that period of success. Built of local limestone with simple Italianate details, these buildings housed a variety of small businesses and offices over the years and still provide a focus for commercial activity in the village.

renamed the Central National Bank) reputed to have been used originally as a store. Simple classical features distinguish this structure. It is remarkable not only for its continuous use as a bank, but for the architectural proportions and details of the projecting entranceway. The keystone arch over the entranceway is surmounted by two pediments, one complete, one broken.

236. THE ALAMO, 33 Main Street, Cherry Valley. In 1865 Abraham Belcher had constructed this magnificent Second Empire mansion originally known as the Belcher residence but more recently known as "The Alamo." The house is a masterpiece, from its broad mansard roof with slate patterning and decorative dormers, and its sophisticated window surrounds, to its centered one-bay porch with seven arches. It stands out as a formal example of the Second Empire period, unusual in a region where the style was normally expressed in less substantial frame structures.

237. CHERRY VALLEY VILLAGE HALL, 44 Main Street, Cherry Valley.
The present village hall was built before 1850 and was known as John Judd's Iron Foundry. Local historians state that one of the first iron plows in New York State was manufactured here. Each community, in its effort to be self-sustaining, developed local products which were commercially successful as long as the major transportation routes continued to cross the region. Cherry Valley had a marble works and melodeon manufacturer (plate 232), Monticello a friction match factory, Elm Grove a chair factory, and Gilbertsville hat and linseed oil factories. As soon as the Erie Canal diverted traffic northward from this part of Central New York economic decline set in.

238. MORSE HOUSE, Montgomery Street, North of Main Street, Cherry Valley.
Samuel F. B. Morse, (1791–1872) came to Cherry Valley in 1837 to visit in this house, the home of his cousin Judge James Morse. Samuel Morse painted while in Cherry Valley, and it was here that he carried out experiments leading to the development in 1843 of the telegraph instrument (plate 232). The Alpha Delta Phi fraternity was also started in this house, which has been owned by the Morse family for many generations. The Morse house has features suggestive of the Federal period, although the entrance portico appears to date from the Greek Revival era.

239. GLENSFOOT, Genesee Street, Cherry Valley. This formal country home at the eastern edge of the village is an elegant Gothic structure, one of the largest in the county. President Martin Van Buren was entertained here in 1838.

9

PRESERVATION IN OTSEGO COUNTY

THIS BOOK WAS PROMPTED by a concern that the rich architectural heritage of Otsego County is unrecognized and undervalued, at the same time that it is increasingly vulnerable to forces of change. Demolition, alteration, neglect, and abandonment are constant threats, all too readily apparent to the interested observer.

The record of landmarks lost is not reassuring. Such major buildings as the County Clerk's Office in Cooperstown, a wonderfully exuberant example of pictorial eclecticism; "Old Main," (plates 25 and 26); the double hop house in Cherry Valley (plate 20); and the commercial sections of Oneonta's Main Street have all been destroyed within the last decade. Other landmarks, less obvious, vernacular structures (but no less important as elements of the landscape), have been abandoned or arbitrarily demolished as well.

While Otsego County reflects preservation problems and trends that exist nationally, it specifically reflects the economic and social problems which contribute to rural underdevelopment. The decline of the dairy industry and the subsequent shrinkage of the rural population have resulted in a widescale abandonment of rural areas and rural structures. In the limited sections of the county where development is occurring, specifically near the southern end of the county where commercial activity and transportation routes are concentrated, the last vestiges of the surrounding rural landscape are being eroded. However, with increased public understanding that architecture is as important in the conservation of an area's identity as the environment is, perhaps Otsego County will develop a deeper commitment to historic preservation.

One argument for preservation is based on the aesthetic appeal of early structural forms as compared with much of our contemporary architectural mediocrity and cluttered surroundings. Visual harmony, excellence of proportion, careful detailing, quality craftsmanship, and durability—all these are in direct contrast to today's typical anonymous, prefabricated structures.

Another argument for preservation concerns the importance of buildings as historic documents. It has only recently been recognized that buildings are important as evidence of traditions and customs, agricultural techniques, settlement patterns, and economic conditions. Otsego County has an abundance of both unusual and typical structures which, both individually and collectively, constitute a three-dimensional record of the county's development. Thus historic resource conservation is essential to maintain these visual links with the past.

The third and perhaps most convincing argument for preservation is that protected and "recycled" buildings may be a critical element in economic revitalization. Adaptive re-use of older buildings, recycled according to local needs, can contribute to the economic vitality of our communities and may bolster a general revitalization of the region.

Historic preservation, therefore, does not imply a sentimental appeal to save one or two gracious mansions. Historic preservation concerns the re-use of the structures which give the county its identity in such a way as to ensure the survival of the natural and physical environment.

There is no easy vehicle for the protection of historic structures. The first step in any such effort is documentation. Much progress has been made in this direction with the survey of Otsego County sites begun in 1971 under the auspices of the New York State Historic Trust (now the Division of Historic Preservation, New York State Parks and Recreation Department) and continued under the auspices of the Upper Catskill Community Council on the Arts and the Otsego County Planning Board. However, such an inventory is useful only if utilized by planners and officials responsible for developing future preservation policies. Fortunately, recent and timely efforts by the Otsego County Planning Office to develop a long-range site inventory and plan indicate growing official awareness of the necessity to plan for historic resource management.

At the local level protective legislation can be the most effective form of historic preservation. Within historic districts or in small communities zoning ordinances or other forms of regulative legislation can be developed.

The protection of individual structures ultimately remains within the hands of individual owners. Historic preservation is possible only when owners develop a sense of pride and responsibility for their own architectural resources. It is to this end that this book is aimed, with the hope that all who enjoy living and traveling in Otsego County will be stimulated to consider the future protection of local landmarks.

240. Barn Cupola, Gilbertsville. Destroyed 1975.

INDEX

Abandoned buildings, 117, 173, 215, 222, 253, 274
Adaptive re-use, 16, 21, 42, 55, 57, 85, 91, 129, 144–45, 190, 197–98, 232, 237, 255–56, 275
Adobe, 2
Agricultural structures, 4, 28–29, 40, 42, 51, 100, 105, 120, 204
A Home for All (Fowler), 197
Alamo, The, 262, 270
Albany, 155, 262, 267
Albany Academy, 44
Albany and Susquehanna Railroad, 86
Albany-Cherry Valley Road, 262
Albert Morris House, 30–31
Allen, Augustus Nicholas, 144
Allen, James, 8
"All Saints Chapel," 2, 124
Alpha Delta Phi, 272
American Builder's Companion, The (Benjamin), 10
American Revolution, 3, 123, 148, 221, 262
Architects and Builders Edition of Scientific American Magazine, 33
Arkwright Cotton Mills, 108
Armory, 183
Armstrong-Stocking House, 167
Auchinbrek, 261
Augustine House, 16

Babb, Cook, and Willard, 88
Baker octagonal barn, 29
Bandstand, 52
Banks, 17, 79, 172, 268–69
Baptist Church, 161
Barber shop, 103
Barnes-Butts House, 191
Barns, 29, 42, 66, 94, 120–21, 204, 222, 225, 246, 260, 276
Barracks, 268

Baseball Hall of Fame, 38, 70
Bates hop house, 268
Beach-Dokuchitz House, 219
Beach, Fred, 5
Beardsley hop house, 109
Beardsley, Levi, 5, 268
Beaux-Arts style, 185–86
Benjamin, Asher, 10, 201
Bicentennial, 138, 186
Bigelow, Henry F., 141
Birdsall, Ralph, 75
Blend, Lyman, 32
Boarding houses, 52. *See also* Hotels; Resorts
Bogardus, James, 78
"Boomtown front," 129
Boston, 137, 141
Brackets, 20, 22, 24, 97, 209, 219, 229
Bresee, Frank, 159
Bresee Store, 159
Bricks, 2, 26, 72–73, 79, 82, 179–80, 193, 207, 213, 236, 241
Brimmer Farm, 176
Brimmer, John, 176
Brimmer, Martha, 176
Buffalo, 262
Builders' guides, 2, 10, 201
Bull House, 25, 179, 197
Bundy, Captain Peter, 202
Bundy Tavern, 202
Burlington Flats, 42, 112–14
Burlington Green, 40
Burlington, Town of, 14, 110, 112–15
Butterfield, Major James, 155–56
Butterfield Tavern, 155
Butternut Creek, 110
Butternut Creek Valley, 96, 111–47
Butternuts, Town of, 110, 134–37
Butternut Valley Arts and Crafts Building, 129
Butter paddle factory, 131

Cabinet shops, 119, 235
Campbell, Col. Samuel, 261
Campbell, James, 261
Canadarago Lake, 43
Canfield Creamery, 213
Canfield, H. Y., 206, 213
Carlyl, Leonard, 236
Carlyl's Store, 236
Carr Homestead, 68
Carriage houses, 58, 88, 244
Carroll House, 257
Cast iron, 78
Catlin Memorial Library, 47
Catskill Turnpike, 3, 204, 207, 220
Central National Bank, 268–69
Central New York, 271
Chapin House, 107
Chapin, John, 107
Charlotte River, 3
Chenango County, 96, 100
Cherry Valley, 3, 12, 28, 41–42, 247, 262–69
Cherry Valley Creek, 247, 262
Cherry Valley Region, 247–73
Cherry Valley, Town of, 247, 260–61
Cherry Valley Village Hall, 271
Chimneys, 4, 10, 154, 157, 191
Christ Church, 75
Churches, 19, 40, 42, 56, 62, 75–76, 115, 117, 126, 138, 142, 161, 201, 233, 253
Civil War, 15, 25, 256–57, 267
Clark, Cyrenus, 8, 75
Clark, Cyrus, 75
Clark, Edward, 258
Clarke, George, 44
Clarke, George Hyde, 44
Clark Foundation, 17
Clinton, General James, 148
Clinton-Sullivan expedition, 148
Cobblestone, 2, 59
Colliersville, 24
Colliscroft, 178

Commercial buildings, 26, 40, 60, 78, 103, 129, 150, 159, 184, 210, 221, 228, 238, 241, 251
Commercial districts, 26, 55, 71, 110, 125, 128, 141, 179, 184, 186, 207–208, 229, 269, 274
Community House, 21
Comstock, William, 163
Connecticut, 113, 125, 172, 208
Construction materials, 2
Construction techniques, 2, 4–5, 10, 13–26, 29–32, 34, 37, 60, 68, 78, 95, 166, 224–25, 238, 260, 275
Cook Homestead, 154
Cooper Inn, 82
Cooper, Isaac, 72
Cooper, James Fenimore, 15, 43, 72, 75, 91, 123
Cooper, William, 3, 77, 155, 202
Cooperstown, 3–4, 6, 8, 17, 23, 25, 33, 38, 42, 70–95, 268
Cooperstown Junction, 86
Cooperstown Municipal Building, 38
Cooperstown and Susquehanna Valley Railroad, 86
Corn crib, 51
Cotton mills, 42, 65, 69, 91
County Clerk's Office, 274
Culley Tavern, 173
Cummings Homestead, 61

Dairy industry, 37, 149, 222, 225, 274
Davis, Jonathan, 132
Davis-Lull House, 132
DeCalvin-Buker Tavern, 204
Decatur, 222
Decatur Creek, 238
Decatur, Township of, 221
Declaration of Independence, 123
Delaware County, 219
Delaware and Hudson Railroad Station, 85
Delaware and Hudson Railway Company Roundhouse, 26
Delos White House, 12, 262
Depot, The, 197

Destroyed buildings, 28, 35, 144–45, 179, 184, 274, 276
Detroit, 203
Division of Historic Preservation, 275
Dr. Greenough House, 2, 151
Doctor's Office, 94, 232
Double hop house, 28, 274
Dow Funeral Home, 81
Draper Academy, 251
Draper, Andrew S., 251
Dutch barn, 260
Dwellings, 4–5, 11, 14, 19, 33, 40, 42, 46, 59, 61, 87, 139, 149, 162–63, 169, 180, 189, 203, 211, 221, 224, 245, 247
Dwight, Dr. Timothy, 207, 220

Early landmarks, 5–6, 46, 61, 176, 179, 181, 247
East Guilford, 204
Eastlake style, 31–32
East Springfield, 48
East Worcester, 222, 226, 231
Economic development, 15, 25, 37, 131, 149, 150, 179, 207, 221, 247, 262–63, 269, 271, 274
Edmeston, 3, 40, 96, 102–104
Edmeston, Town of, 96, 102–105
Educational buildings, 35, 40, 140, 145, 153
Elm Grove, 271
Elnathan Noble House, 116
Emerson, William Ralph, 137, 147
Emigrés, 125
Emmons, 177, 202
Emmons, Ira, 177
Environmental features, 4, 39–40, 42, 52–53, 70, 110–11, 113, 133, 136, 147, 207, 247–48, 263, 274–75
Erie Canal, 15, 40, 271
Europe, 24, 34, 180, 185
Exeter Center, 60–61
Exeter, Town of, 43, 59–63

Fairchild, George W., 194
Fairchild Mansion, 194
Fancher Home, 212
Fancher, Selek H., 212
Farmers' Museum, 4, 92–95, 160
Farmhouses, 6, 14, 43, 149, 158, 164, 182, 203, 221
Federal style, 10–12, 43, 73, 98, 118, 126, 135, 170, 202, 221, 226, 231
Fenimore Cooper's Grave and Christ Churchyard (Birdsall), 75
Fenimore House, 65
Ferry, Dexter M., 203
Ferry Mansion, 203
Fields, W. C., 163
Filer's Corners, 92
Firehouses, 131, 242
First Congregational Church, 117
First National Bank Building, 79
"Five Sisters," 102
Flagg, Ernest, 38
Fly Creek, 40, 44, 66–67
Forestview, 33
Fort Alden, 262
Fort Stanwix Treaty, 3
Foundry, 271
Fowler, Orson Squire, 197
Franchot, Judge Pascal, 126
Francis Carriage Works, 49
Franklin, 219
Freight house, 215
Fuller, Albert, 35
Fuller and Wheeler, 35
Funeral homes, 57, 81

Gardner House, 164
Garrattsville, 110, 121
Gatehouses, 44, 133
Gazlay Farm, 105
Gazlay, Jacob, 105

Georgian style, 4, 7–9, 61, 74, 105, 126, 154
Gilbert Block, 141
Gilbert Homestead, 144
Gilbert, Joseph T., 145
Gilbert, Major James L., 144
Gilbertsville, 20, 40–41, 110, 123, 134, 136–47, 271
Gilbertsville Academy and Collegiate Institute, 145
Gilbertsville Free Library, 140
Gilbertsville Grange Hall, 142, 201
Gilbertsville Post Office, 142
Gladstone Building, 55
Glensfoot, 273
"Glimmerglass," 43
Goddard, Edward, 226
Goddard House, 226
Gothic Revival Style, 18–19, 56, 75, 107, 109, 115, 124, 132, 180, 201, 217, 244, 253–54, 273
Gould, Frank, 193
Gould-Kellogg House, 193
Grablewyn, 231
Grange Hall (Gilbertsville), 138
Granite, 2, 186, 188
Great Britain, 1, 41
Greater Milford Historical Society, 170
Great Western Turnpike, 262
Greece, 13
Greek Revival Style, 13–17, 40, 43–44, 63, 110, 116, 133, 151, 158, 160, 167, 169, 182, 198, 211, 221, 236, 245, 251
Greene County, 170
Griggs Store, 251
Griswold, Elijah, 231
Griswold House, 231
"Grove, The," 44, 133

Hamilton College Chapel, 44
Harrieff House, 193
Harrington House, 20
Hartwick, 3, 92, 148–49, 160–62

Hartwick College, 179
Hartwick, Town of, 151–62
Hayes House, 220
Herkimer, George, 63
Herkimer House, 63
Hemstreet-Pendleton House, 193
Hinman Hollow, 92
Historic districts, 41–42, 70–90, 136–45, 148, 180, 189–93, 207, 238–46, 276
Historic resource conservation, 275–76
Historic sites inventory, 275
Hoboken Corners, 108–109
Holden Inn, 157
Holden, Stephen, 157
Home as Found (Cooper), 13, 15
Hooker, Philip, 4, 46
Hops, 25, 28, 109, 149, 152, 158, 177, 193, 268
Hotel Bishop, 217
Hotels, 52, 54–55, 89, 179, 185, 217
Housewrights, 1, 10
Hudson River, 207, 268
Huntington, Collis P., 178
Hyde Hall, 44

Immanuel Protestant Episcopal Church, 201
Index, 69, 151
Indians, 3, 207
Industrial buildings, 40, 42, 44, 65, 69, 110, 114, 131, 149, 213–14, 237, 271
International Business Machines (IBM), 194
Interstate-88, 150, 222
Ironclad Building, 78
Italianate style, 20–22, 101, 174, 209, 222

Johnston-Wood House, 74
Judd, John, 271

Kahn, Albert, 203

Kellogg, A. L., 193
Keyes-Tipple House, 226
Keyes, Washington, 226
Kingfisher Tower, 258

Lakelands, 71
Lake Region, 43–95
Landmarks, ix, 4, 39–42, 70–71, 96–97, 111–12, 136–37, 148–50, 179–80, 184, 207–208, 221–22, 247–48, 258, 262, 274–76
Laurens, 16, 40, 148–49, 163, 165
Laurens, Town of, 163–70
Leatherstocking Corporation, 17
Leatherstocking Tales (Cooper), 43
The Legends and Traditions of a Northern County (Cooper), 9
Lena, 120
Libraries, 38, 47, 140, 232
"Lily Vale," 212
Limestone, 2, 43, 49, 188, 269
Lincoln, Abraham, 202
Lippitt Farmhouse, 6, 92
Literary Institute, 251
Lithia Springs Pavilion, 262
Log barn, 95
Log structures, 4–5, 95, 175
"Longhouse Museum," 179
Louisville, 125
Lumber, 177, 220

McCormick Cottage, 58
McCormick, Cyrus, 58
McGrath Funeral Home, 57
McKim House, 88
McKim, Mead and White, 58
Madison County, 96
Major's Inn, 136, 141, 144
Manor houses, 44, 123
Mansard, François, 23

Mansard roofs, 23, 25, 83, 106, 197, 270
Maplehurst, 16
Maples, David, 158
Maples, Louise, 158
Maples Homestead, 158
Martin Noble Cabinet Shop, 119
Martin Noble House, 118
Maryland, 222, 224–25
Maryland, Town of, 5, 221
Masonic Hall (Cooperstown), 90
Masonic Temple (Oneonta), 194
Masons, 90, 194, 257, 266
Massachusetts, 202
Massacre of 1778, 261–62
Mayall, Joseph, 166
Mayall-Powell House, 166
Meeker House, 219
Meridian Sun Lodge, 118
Methodist Church, 223, 253
Middlefield, 92, 94, 248, 256–57
Middlefield Center, 257
Middlefield Historical Association, 256
Middlefield, Town of, 247, 254–58
Milfer Farm, 203
Milford, 25, 170–73
Milford Center, 175
Milford National Bank, 172
Milford, Town of, 171–75
Milfordville, 182
Miller Tavern, 7
Mills, 42, 65, 67, 69, 108, 110, 114, 149, 221
Mineral springs, 262
Mohawk River, 247, 262
Mohawk Valley, 13, 43, 247
Monticello, 7, 44, 271
Monument Square, 266
Moody House, 189
Moore House, 193
Morris, 3, 11, 41–42, 110, 125–33, 229
Morris, General Jacob, 123–26
Morris, James, 12, 272

Morris, Lewis, 103
Morris Manor, 123
Morris Manor Chapel, 124
Morris, Richard, 123
Morris, Town of, 11, 122–33
Morse House, 272
Morse, S. F. B., 266–67, 272
Mount Upton, 135
Mount Vision, 168–70
Mumford, Col. Alfred, 175
Museums, 70, 91–95, 179, 198

National Register of Historic Places, 136, 148, 188, 194
Nelson Lewis Wagon Shop, 122
Neo-Classical Revival style, 37–38, 172, 178, 186, 188–89, 193, 226
Neo-Tudor style, 136, 141, 144
New Berlin, 97, 101, 109
New England, 1, 10, 40, 96, 147, 208
New Jersey, 3, 125
New Lisbon, 11, 110, 116–19
New Lisbon, Town of, 116–21
New York Archaeological Association, 198
New York State, 2, 10, 18, 169, 275
New York State Historical Association, 91
New York State Historic Trust, 275
New York State Legislature, 3
New York State Parks and Recreation Department, 275
Noble, Elnathan, 116
Noble, George H., 211
Noble, Martin, 118–19
Noble-Sands House, 211
Noblesville, 116, 118
North, Col. S. S., 209
North-Lyon House, 209

Oaksville, 64–66
Oakwood, 265
Octagonal buildings, 25, 29, 121, 197, 212
Old Main, 34–35, 179, 274
Old Middlefield Schoolhouse, 256
Old Post Office Building, 180, 188
Old Smithy, 77
Old Stone Church, 62
Olmstead, Frederick Law, 58
Oneonta, City of, 25, 32, 35–37, 179–97
Oneonta Hotel, 185
Oneonta Municipal Building, 180, 186–87
Oneonta Normal School, 35, 179
Oneonta, Town of, 176–97
Orange County, 3
Otego, 149, 198–202
Otego Creek, 148
Otego Presbyterian Church, 138, 201
Otego Valley Grange, 170
Otesaga Hotel, 89
Otsego Cotton Mill, 149, 163
Otsego County, 1–4, 10, 13, 15, 18–21, 23, 25, 30–32, 34, 37, 39–42, 125, 158, 274–76
Otsego County Bank, 17, 44, 268
Otsego County Courthouse, 84
Otsego County Jail, 83
Otsego County Planning Board, 275
Otsego Lake, 43, 70, 72, 91, 148, 258
Otsego, Town of, 3, 198–202
Ouleout Creek, 207
"Overlook," 145

Palladian window, 10–11, 118, 126, 208
Palmer-Hunt House, 198
Pardee, Edmund, 178
Parks, 44, 52–53, 70, 124, 137, 142, 145, 181, 206, 219

Patents, 3, 110
Pearse, George, 154
Pegg House, 11
Pennsylvania, 148
Phillips, Parley, 98
Pictorial Eclectic style, 30–31, 40, 193
Pinney, Joshua L., 257
Pinney's Tavern, 257
Pittsfield, 96
Pittsfield, Town of, 96, 106–110
Plainfield, Town of, 96–101
Pomeroy, George, 8
Pomeroy Place, 8–9
Population, Otsego Co., 10, 13, 37, 39, 42, 44, 110, 149, 179
Portlandville, 174
Powell, Isaac, 163, 166
Presbyterian Church, 76
Preservation, 39, 42, 70, 121, 150, 179, 180, 190, 248, 274–76
Preston House, 175
Price, William, 257
Proctor Place, 160
Proctor, Thomas R., 53, 56
Public buildings, 37, 40, 141, 172, 180, 184, 186, 188, 222

Queen Anne style, 32–33, 40, 150, 162, 190, 193

Railroad, 26, 28, 30, 40, 96, 149–50, 179, 221, 240, 247
Railroad structures, 26, 85–86, 104, 169, 179, 197, 215
Recycled buildings, 275
Referential buildings, 1, 30, 37, 44, 185–86
Reminiscences (Beardsley), 5
Resorts, 43–44, 52, 54, 89, 145, 206
Richardson, H. H., 34
Richardsonian style, 34, 147, 183
Richfield Springs, 40, 52–58
Richfield, Town of, 29, 51

Richied Place, 106
River Street Primary School, 36
Roads, 7, 149–50, 202, 221, 247, 262, 264, 274
Rockwell brothers, 138, 201
Roland B. Hill Archaeological Museum, 198
Romanesque style, 34–36, 79, 142, 147, 183
Roseboom, 247
Roseboom, Town of, 247–249
Rotch, Francis, 133
Rotch Mansion, 44, 133
Route 20, 44, 48–50, 52, 55–56
Rowe House, 189
Rowley-Sloan Residence, 243
Rural structures, 37, 42–43, 96, 110–11, 149, 153, 222, 247, 274
Russell, Archimedes, 84

St. John's Episcopal Church, 56
St. Matthew's Episcopal Church, 217
Saltbox style, 4, 134, 181
Saratoga Springs, 202
Sayre, David, 170
Sayre House, 170
Schenevus, 40, 221–22, 226–31
Schenevus Creek, 221, 238
Schenevus Creek Valley, 221–47
Schools, 35, 42, 48, 145, 153, 222, 251, 256
Schuyler Lake, 63
Scotch Jamie, 8, 68
Second Empire style, 23–24, 31, 54, 83, 180, 189, 270
Settlement patterns, 3, 39, 43, 96, 125, 149, 207, 275
Settlers, 5–6, 10, 113, 125, 136, 155, 261, 262
Seward, William, 202
Shingle style, 32–33, 88, 147
Sidney, 204
Silvernail barn, 204
Skaneateles Turnpike, 7
Smith, Captain Dan, 125, 133
Smith House, 189

Smith and Swartout Building, 241
Smokehouses, 105
Solon Benedict House, 134
Southern Pacific Railroad, 178
South Hartwick, 159
South Valley, 247
South Worcester, 224, 232–35
Springfield, 49–50
Springfield Center, 46–47, 257
Springfield, Town of, 43–50
Springhouse Park, 52–53
Stables, 58, 80, 194, 221, 246
Stag's Head Inn, 145
Stansfield Villa, 54
State University of New York at Oneonta, 35
Steere, Ira, 71
Steere, Rufus, 64
Steere, Squire, 69
Stick style, 31, 57, 103, 129, 242, 246
Stone, 2, 43–44, 60, 63–64, 68, 125, 133, 135, 142, 145, 177, 183, 203, 207, 231, 237, 249, 268
Stone meetinghouse, 113
Stone mill, 237
Stylistic analysis, 1, 25, 180, 221
Sullivan, General John, 148
Summers House, 23
Susquehanna River, 3, 41, 43, 148, 158, 206–207, 219, 221
Swan, Amos, 266–67
Swart-Wilcox House, 179, 181
Syracuse, 267

Taverns, 4, 154–55, 157, 173, 202, 204, 257
Telegraph, 266–67, 272
Temple form, 15, 17, 169, 234, 249
Thrall, Freeborn D., 160
Tianderah, 137, 147, 206
Tiffany, Louis Comfort, 56
Toddsville, 18, 44, 68, 92, 152

Tollhouse, 264
Transitional buildings, 15, 25, 108, 126, 165, 191, 201, 221, 224, 233
Transportation, 40, 149, 221, 274
Trinity Parish, 217
Turnpikes, 7, 202, 204, 207, 247, 262
Twin houses, 73

Unadilla, 3, 21–22, 25–26, 40, 42, 202, 207–220
Unadilla Center, 203
Unadilla Forks, 96–98
Unadilla River, 3, 96, 101, 110, 135, 148, 207, 219
Unadilla Silo, 214
Unadilla, Town of, 203–220
Underground Railroad, 151
Underwood Brothers, 99, 106
University of Illinois, 251
Upper Catskill Community Council on the Arts, 275
Upper Catskill Mountains, 148
Upper Susquehanna Chapter of the New York Archaeological Association, 198
Upper Susquehanna River Basin, 148–220, 247, 268
Upper Unadilla Valley, 96–110

Van Buren, Martin, 255, 273
Van Rensselaer House, 126
Van Rensselaer, Jacob, 126
Vernacular buildings, 1–2, 10–11, 21, 43, 70–71, 87, 93–94, 99, 103, 110, 115, 135–36, 139, 148, 155, 161, 165, 170, 175, 206–207, 224, 233, 243, 249, 251, 274
Victorian period, 25, 40, 54, 96–97, 106, 150, 180, 194, 221, 225
Village Crossroads, 92–95, 160
Village development, 30, 39–41, 52–53, 79, 110–11, 113–14, 125, 149, 179, 207, 221–22, 226, 247, 262, 266

Wagonshops, 49, 122, 257
Wallbridge brothers, 113–14
Walnut Street Historic District, 41–42, 148, 189–93
Washington, George, 261
"Wattle's Ferry," 207
Welcome, 120
Wellhouses, 168, 204
West Burlington, 115
Westcott Building, 158
West Exeter, 25, 59
Westford, 92, 94, 247, 251–53
Westford, Town of, 247, 251–53
Wharton Creek, 113–14
Wharton Valley, 104
Wharton Valley Line, 104
Wheeler House, 24
White House, 155, 208
Whiting, Frank P., 72
Wightman Building, 238
Wilber, George I., 190
Wilber Mansion, 190
Wilcox, Henry, 98
Williams Corners, 100
Williams House, 99
Willowbrook, 82
Wood, 2, 43, 169, 180, 207
Woodside Hall, 255
Woolworth Building, 184
Worcester, 3, 41, 221–22, 231, 235, 237–46
Worcester Historic District, 40, 238–46
Worcester, Town of, 221
Wright, Roswell, 219
Wyandotte (Cooper), 68, 123

Yager Collection of Indian Artifacts, 179
Yager House, 182
Yager, Willard E., 179
Yale College, 207
York Corporation, 208, 213

Zion Episcopal Church, 126
Zoning, 275–76

Landmarks of Otsego County

was composed in twelve-point Merganthaler VIP Bodoni Book and leaded one point,
with display type in Poster Bodoni by Utica Typesetting Company, Inc.;
and published by

SYRACUSE UNIVERSITY PRESS
SYRACUSE, NEW YORK 13244-5290

www.ingramcontent.com/pod-product-compliance
Lightning Source LLC
Chambersburg PA
CBHW050457110426
42742CB00018B/3288